Can God Use Me?

Can God Use Me?

Turning Your Weaknesses into His Opportunities

Robert Amess

Hodder & Stoughton
LONDON SYDNEY AUCKLAND

First published in Great Britain in 2000

The right of Robert Amess to be identified as the Author of
the Work has been asserted by him in accordance
with the Copyright, Designs and Patents Act 1988.

10 9 8 7 6 5 4 3 2 1

British Library Cataloguing in Publication Data
A record for this book is available from the British Library

ISBN 0 340 74634 3

Typeset by Avon Dataset Ltd, Bidford-on-Avon, Warks

Printed and bound in Great Britain by
The Guernsey Press Co. Ltd, Channel Isles

Hodder & Stoughton
A Division of Hodder Headline Ltd
338 Euston Road
London NW1 3BH

To June

Contents

Foreword

I knew I would like this book, but I was not prepared for how much — it is absolutely terrific. It has to be one of the most encouraging writings to emerge from the press in many years. So many Christians today feel inadequate, unsure of their calling and are largely devoid of a sense of destiny — all because of what they perceive in themselves as a lack of gifting or adequate personality. This book will help lay such fears to rest.

While this is a no-nonsense book, Robert's wry sense of humour comes out on nearly every page. I found myself laughing out loud all the time. It is down-to-earth, very easy to read, and will hold your attention from the beginning. But it is also quite sobering in places, as when he says, 'My fear is that in Britain today God is doing something that we neither expected nor wanted: he is judging us' (p. 29). There is also a surprising prophetic note that will stimulate you and give pause for reflection again and again. Best of all, it is so very, very encouraging.

Pastors and vicars will find a lot of fresh sermon material in what follows. I hope they will pass this on to their members. But people in the pew are the ones for whom this book is mainly designed.

Now Chairman of the Evangelical Alliance and currently the Moderator of the Eden Baptist Church in Cambridge, Robert has been the Senior Minister of Duke Street Baptist Church in Richmond for the past thirteen years. He is in wide demand as a preacher and conference speaker both in the British Isles and in remote places in the world. I have, however, warned Robert that Jesus said, 'Woe unto you when all speak well of you' – Robert seems to have no enemies!

Robert and Beth Amess have been our closest friends in Britain. They are God's gifts to Louise and me. A true friend is someone who knows all about you and *still* likes you! Robert calls himself 'the complete loner'. He is so 'English' that I find it continually intriguing that he wants someone like me for his friend! I only know that we have laughed and cried together through joys and sorrows over the years, whether it be having coffee or lunch in my vestry, or the four of us having fish and chips at Geale's in Notting Hill Gate. Robert and Beth have provided the outlet we have needed so often to be ourselves without having to wear a mask.

You will be glad you own this book. It will make a difference in your life. I commend it to you and trust that it will be widely read throughout Britain and the world.

R. T. Kendall
Westminster Chapel, London

Introduction

Here is an odd thing. God seems to find pleasure in using the most unlikely people for his purposes. In fact, whenever you turn to Scripture, church history, biography or autobiography, you keep bumping into people you would never imagine that God would be interested in, let alone use. In the final instance, only he knows why imperfect people are chosen – but I have an idea as to why this should be, and this is what I want to share in this book. I have come to the conclusion that since all of us have one sort of flaw or another, it stands to reason that God can *only* use people (*with*) problems! Since 'all have sinned', most sensitive souls probably suspect that they are discounted from God's service, but God does not seem to be deterred by that. Perhaps that does not sound very profound, but who said anything about being profound?

One day, when I was studying at Spurgeon's College, I was looking around at members of my fellow year-group who were training for the ordained ministry. We were a close group and had grown to know each other well. I was thinking that we hardly seemed to be the sort of material that God would, or could, use. Not many of us seemed highly gifted, or likely to make a great impact for Christ and his Church. Yet that was well over thirty years ago now, and some of those apparently very ordinary students have become highly significant in the kingdom of God. We have been taken by God and developed into something significant, however small our potential seemed.

And, rather encouragingly – or perhaps disappointingly, depending on how you look at it – the opposite has frequently been true as well. Over the years I have often met humanly gifted people, and even spiritually gifted people, whom I had presumed were clearly marked out for great things. But in fact time has shown that they have made little impact in God's kingdom, and for one reason or another have discounted or disqualified themselves from his service.

I suppose this could be a reason why often seemingly unpromising people (from a human perspective, that is) have been the ones who have achieved most for God. For, rather than having any illusions about themselves, God has surprised them by his grace in choosing them for his work. But in the final analysis, it is all very puzzling. In fact, some of us will live with the puzzle till our dying day. That is the conundrum and, in a nutshell, it is what this book is about and the reason why I have written it. It is addressed to unlikely people who ask the vital question 'Could God use *me*?'

Now all this is not just my theory, for Scripture seems to indicate that most (if not all) of the characters in the Bible appeared to be unsuitable – for one reason or another – for God's purposes. Yet God *did* use these people. I find this to be a tremendous encouragement and hope that you do too.

Although this book only draws on Old Testament

characters, I would not like you to imagine that this is just an Old Testament phenomenon. We come to the same conclusion when we look at the inadequacies of Jesus's disciples, or at some of the problems that Paul had to face on his missionary journeys – not only problems with himself, but also with those who accompanied him. The members of the New Testament churches seemed quite a collection of dysfunctional people, bearing in mind the amount of letter-writing needed to try and sort them out! I repeat: it is quite clear that God calls into his Church, and then uses, the most unlikely people for his glory.

Paul delights in pointing out to the church at Corinth that God makes a speciality of calling ordinary people into his service. 'Not many of you were wise or influential', he said; in fact, he tells them, God chooses the foolish, weak, lowly and despised things to shame the wise and strong (1 Cor. 1:26–8). Paul also tells us that God does this so that 'no-one may boast before him' (1 Cor. 1:29).

The solemn truth is that for the ones who imagine they have much to offer God, who think that they are pretty essential for the well-being of the kingdom of God, they are going to be passed by, superb gifting or not. The reason is this: God is never going to 'give [his] glory to another' (Isa. 42:8). That is why nearly all the Bible characters that I can think of were surprised that God had deigned to use them. The common testimony of this motley crew was that rather than boasting in themselves, they boasted 'in the Lord' (1 Cor. 1:31).

King David is a case in point. To say that he was surprised after his moral disasters that God could use him again is quite an understatement. Quite rightly so, we might think, in view of what we know of his life. Yet God thought differently. David said, 'my sin is always before me' (Ps. 51:3), and we take some perverse satisfaction in that. 'You're finished, you're perm-anently disqualified' would be our verdict on David; but it was not God's verdict, for he restored him.

Incidentally, there are some people in the Church today who feel that whereas this might have been true for David, because it clearly says so in the Bible, it is certainly not possible for those who have sinned today. Somehow, they believe, David was a special exception and that people now are different. This is very strange, and wrong thinking, for God deals with people today in the same way as he did then. That is God's nature: he does not change.

Paul described himself as the 'chief of sinners', and he had a point. Many of us might perhaps consider that assisting in the martyrdom of an apostle was as good a reason as any to be written out of the plan of God – not counting the unrecorded Christians who probably died because he had had them thrown into prison. But God does not work like that. I say with the hymn-writer (I often do, it's a weakness of mine), 'O how the grace of God amazes me'.

God is still David's God. The way he dealt with Paul is still the divine method. I firmly believe that there are many Christians who for one reason or another are saying, 'God can't use me', but are forgetting what God has done with the most unlikely of people and the most dreadful of sinners.

One of my hobbies, when I have time, is model-making. Do you remember programmes like *Blue Peter* where the unlikely materials were assembled – cardboard from toilet rolls, matchboxes, washing-up liquid bottles, etc. – to make some-thing that sounded very grand and looked even better? At a given moment, the presenters put their hands under the table and said those magic words: 'Here's one I made earlier.' This is what this book is about. It demonstrates what God 'did earlier' with the most unlikely collection of people, in making them usable in his service. I have an absolute conviction that he can do the same with you and me today.

Now don't misunderstand me. I will not be arguing that either the sinful or the second-rate are the qualities that God is looking for in people today. Far from it! A desire for personal holiness is essential if we are to be effective for God. There should be a holy ambition to become what God wants us to be. We want to be as usable for God as we can be, whether we have an overt ministry or not. I certainly believe in gifting. I also support training; as a past chairman of a Bible college I have given a lot of my time to improving its value and relevance for service. Nevertheless, this book will argue that *all* of us are the people God uses, whatever our history or lack of opportunity for training.

The tragedy that is addressed here is the countless number of people I have met, often reflected in myself, who say that because of family background, lack of formal education, social mishap, past failure or whatever, they are discounted from being used by God. But that is not true. In fact, it is a lie of the devil. Of the biblical characters we will be looking at, one could have said, 'I was brought up in a problem family', another, 'No one understands me', another, 'But I am not gifted', while yet another felt that no one liked him. And although these cries from the heart are true to one degree or another, Scripture records that these very same men and women were of significance in the purposes of God. One of the reasons they are found in Scripture is for our encouragement, just as I trust this book will be an encouragement to you. Not every situation described will meet each individual need, but I hope the cumulative effect will be of relevance to us all.

It is my intention that this book should be simple, sometimes painfully simple, so that it can be easily understood by all. I am not presenting a research thesis for examination, but instead writing something that I hope will meet personal needs and longings. I want to speak to the many Christians I have met who have either been disqualified by others, or have disqualified themselves, from the hope of being significant for God.

Equally intentionally, and perhaps more controversially, I have drawn on personal experiences of life and ministry to illustrate what I am trying to say. I feel it is important to reiterate that we are all real people who are living ordinary lives on pilgrimage. Together we are becoming the people God uses.

1

I do not know where I am going: Abraham's story

There is one question that a minister dreads more than any other, and it will help if I put it into its context. About every eighteen months or so a well-meaning person would come to my vestry and ask with much solemnity and earnestness, 'Where is this church going?' It's a killer of a question for several obvious reasons. I could have answered it with the appropriate 'spiritual' platitudes that the professional training of a minister can conjure up as required. Or, if I dared, with something like, 'Funny you should ask that, because to be quite frank it's not where the church is going that is worrying me at the moment. My problem is that I don't know where *I* am going.'

If you find that rather shocking, so be it, but in leaping to my defence I would point out that I am in good company, for this was the experience of Abraham. Scripture says quite explicitly that he too did not know where he was going. This apparent lack of direction was not caused by some fogginess as to the will of God, or lack of direction from the Holy Spirit, or by personal antagonism to the will of God. Abraham's problem, if that is what it was, sprang from his simple obedience to the express command of God. He was 'called to go . . . even though he did not know where he was going' (Heb. 11:8). It could not be stated more baldly than that.

Of course, Abraham's qualification for greatness was not his ignorance of direction – if it had been, many of us would also be giants of the faith. Abraham's secret was plain obedience to the naked word of God, and that is what most of us find a little more difficult. He had a simple faith, which believed that God meant what he said and never teased. When God said, 'go to the land I will show you' (Gen. 12:1), that was enough for Abraham and he went (Gen. 12:4). Yet when Abraham was faced with the concerned enquiries of family and dependants as to where they were going, he could only reply, 'I don't know.'

My wife and I have had a few glimpses of this sort of faith over the years. When Duke Street Baptist Church, Richmond, called us to leave the stability and joy of our ministry in Ipswich I had little comprehension of where we were going or what it would involve other than that it would be difficult. When we informed Helen, our eldest daughter – who was then fourteen, and at a critical stage in her education – she asked if we were being serious. Having ascertained that we were deadly serious, she coldly informed us that we had ruined her life. We could offer no assurance as to the future other than that we believed that this was what God wanted us to do.

This sort of obedience is described in the Bible as faith. Faith comes in different shapes and sizes in the Bible and for different situations. It is faith in the work of Christ on the cross that saves us (Rom. 10:9). It is that realisation that we cannot add anything to what God has done through Christ for our salvation, and that we can do no other than accept it with repentance and faith. Faith is also described as a gift of the Spirit (1 Cor. 12:9), and is closer to the sort of faith I am talking about here. Christian history is littered with people like Abraham, who seem to have a special, extraordinary faith for specific tasks. People like George Muller, Hudson Taylor and Gladys Aylward. If these names are foreign to you, then read some Christian biographies and start with these people. When I have discovered that others before me have, by the grace of God, faced and overcome some of the things I am going through, this has been a tremendous encouragement.

For Abraham, faith seemed to have its primary expression in leaving the question of destination with God and to trust him for the future. It is as a man of faith that Abraham is described as the father of us all (Rom. 4:16–17). The young people at my church in Ipswich used to sing a chorus that I had to ban in the end. The trouble was not the words, but the actions that went with it – a sort of hokey-kokey that became very disruptive! The words of the chorus were:

> Father Abraham had many sons.
> I am one, so are you, so
> Let's all praise the Lord!

That can only be true of us if we, like Abraham, not only trust him theoretically for future direction, but have actually set out on the journey.

But it was not a blind faith. As Abraham's caravan of camels, family and servants wound its way across the desert, they may not have been sure where they were going, but they could look back and see where they had come from. Their footprints were markers along the way. The most significant pointer of all was God's specific command to Abraham to go on pilgrimage. He must have looked back to that constantly. For myself, I have invariably found it easier to look back and see the hand of God at work in my life than to know what lies ahead. Ahead is the open ocean of life with all its unknowns and imponderables, but the past tells a different story for the believer. As the hymn-writer says:

> His love in time past forbids me to think
> He'll leave me at last in trouble to sink.

This year has seen the coming of a new millennium. As chairman of the Evangelical Alliance, my wife and I had the privilege of being invited to attend the National Service for the millennium at St Paul's Cathedral in the presence of the Queen and Prime Minister. The Archbishop of Canterbury preached helpfully on being pilgrims. He drew from Bunyan's great hymn on pilgrimage, 'He who would true valour see'. You will remember Bunyan's story of Christian's journey to the Promised Land in *Pilgrim's Progress*. What carried Christian forward? It was the command of the Evangelist to set out, with his scroll to teach and guide him, and a sword to defend himself. If he had known the terrible dangers that lay ahead, perhaps he would never have started his journey, but the command to go forward was sufficient to bring him eventually to the Celestial City.

Honesty demands that I cannot amaze you by testifying to dramatic instances of future guidance, but I can tell you how I got to where I am at the moment. I suppose the most important thing I ever did (after being born) was to get married. Can I say I was led into that? Well, I certainly fell hopelessly in love with my wife if that is the same thing. Then our much-loved children sort of arrived! Of next importance, I think, were the churches where I have had the privilege to minister. They all 'called' me, for I certainly didn't apply! There have been too many occasions when I have been in the right place at the right time for it to be a coincidence. How many funerals have I taken where I have been able to say I had visited in the twenty-four hours or so before that person died? How many times has a sermon been just the word to meet someone's particular need?

The most dramatic sense of leading I ever had was my call to the ministry. I was driving home for lunch one day when God spoke to me. I can't tell you how, any more than I can tell you how God spoke to Abraham (he of course had no Scripture, and God was in the habit of speaking audibly in those days). I did not hear an audible voice, but on that day I knew that I had met with God. Over a period of three or four months through prayer, Scripture reading and the witness of friends, God gave me such a sense of call, that had it not been so clear I would have taken no notice. What is more, that sense of divine intervention and commission has never been taken away.

'But all that is personal to you', I can hear you protest, and in protesting you have made my point exactly. God meets with us differently. No one life is a blueprint for another. Isaiah confirms this in speaking of Abraham. He says, 'look to Abraham, your father . . . When I called him he was but one' (Isa. 51:2). That can be translated, 'He was alone.' God always speaks to people one at a time. You might be in a great congregation, but there comes that realisation that God is speaking only to you. In the course of an ordinary life comes the realisation that God is trying to say something specifically to us as individuals.

Brian Mawhinney, in his recent autobiography *In the Firing Line* (Marshall Pickering, 1999), has been derided by some for writing that while he was praying in Peterborough Cathedral God called him into politics. I do not doubt Brian for a moment. For many of us, when on those rare occasions God has spoken, we know full well that he has. And some of us have spent the rest of our lives on the strength of that calling, not necessarily anticipating that such an event would happen again.

But Abraham had a problem that is common to most of us. The call of God was vague. 'Leave . . . and go to the land I will show you' is hardly spelling it out (Gen. 12:1). Nevertheless, he went, for that is the very essence of this 'not knowing where you are going' business. Abraham was not told where 'the land' was until he got there.

When I was a boy I was a fanatical reader of C. S. Forester's Hornblower series. Perhaps these books, and those of Arthur Ransome, is where my love of the sea came from. You will remember that Hornblower was often instructed by the Admiralty to travel to such and such a chart reference, then he had to open his sealed orders and go on from there. That is how it was with Abraham, and how it is to be with us. All that is necessary for the obedient Christian is to take the next step –

I do not ask to see the distant scene,
One step enough for me

– says J. H. Newman. Charles Wesley put it like this when speaking of the Children of Israel crossing the desert to the Promised Land:

We shall not *full* direction need,
Nor miss our providential way.

And that must be true for all those who set out on pilgrimage
at the command of God. But all this raises certain objections.
How can I trust God? What if I end up somewhere I do not
want to be? How will I know when I get there? Now I will
be struggling to answer that last question, so let's deal with
the first two to start with.

To help Abraham, God gave him a promise – in fact, over
the course of his life he gave him several. 'I will make you
into a great nation and I will bless you; I will make your name
great, and you will be a blessing . . . and all peoples on earth
will be blessed through you' (Gen. 12:2–3). I don't know
what Abraham made of this talk of being made 'a great nation',
but it could not have meant too much at the time. You can
imagine Abraham telling God that he needed something a
little more concrete for now – something to be going on
with. And yet whether we like it or not, there is a rule here
for those who want to be led by God.

Many centuries after Abraham there was an occasion when
the disciples asked Jesus this understandable question. Since
we have left wives and jobs to follow you, 'What then will
there be for us?' (Matt. 19:27). They wanted something
tangible to hang on to, some present evidence that they were
blessed of God. But Jesus was none too pleased, for all the
promises of God are about the future – otherwise, they would
not of course be *promises* but present realities. Dr Martyn
Lloyd-Jones spoke of 'penny in the slot Christianity'. 'Penny
in the slot Christianity' is to have the expectation that because
I have done something for God I can expect an immediate
reward from him. In other words, because I have put my penny

in the slot I can expect a bar of chocolate in the tray below. But for Abraham and us, the promises are future ones and we have to wait. To the complaint 'but I don't know where I am going' comes the uncomfy reply 'set out on the journey first and I will show you'.

To the second and legitimate question, 'But how will I know the way?', comes the sometimes frustrating reply (I almost used the word *tantalising*, but remember God does not tease), 'I will show you'. There are several New Testament promises to confirm this. The New Testament has a definition of faith. It is 'Now faith is being sure of what we hope for and certain of what we do not see' (Heb. 11:1). Paul confirms this when he says, 'We live by faith, not by sight' (2 Cor. 5:7), and remember Jesus's immortal words to Thomas, 'blessed are those who have not seen and yet have believed' (John 20:29).

Sadly, this truth has been abused frequently and there needs to be an important caveat here. The abuse is what is called 'pie in the sky by and by when I die' Christianity – yet it is not Christianity at all, for it has to do with keeping many people poor and disadvantaged in this life by painting a rosy picture of some uncertain future. It has meant that people have been kept in slavery with the promises of riches in heaven. They have been refused their human rights because they have a home 'above the bright blue sky'. This is not what the Bible means. Listen to some of the Negro spirituals. They talk about walking in shoes 'all over God's heaven' which implies that it will pan out all right in the end, but 'there ain't no shoes now'. Listen to some frustrated, ill-used soul who is told to grin and bear it, for there is a reward in heaven but not before.

This sort of teaching, so prevalent in an earlier age, can sound like a carrot before a donkey to drag us onward and keep us from complaining. In fact Abraham was given many blessings from God along the journey, but they did not deflect him from pursuing the ultimate prize – namely, the country that God had promised. That is why he is called the 'father of all who believe' (Rom. 4:11). The only property he ever owned was a piece of ground in which he could be buried. He was constantly looking for something better, yet God was giving to him every day. God satisfied Abraham's physical, intellectual and emotional needs, but these were not an end in themselves for they pointed forward.

A teacher once asked a class what faith was. 'Believing that which you know isn't true' came the reply. But Christians are never asked to commit intellectual suicide for what they believe – nor dare they. At the moment I have responsibility for a church in Cambridge that jokes that you need a PhD to use the overhead projector. The point is that there are many distinctly clever people around who are also professing Bible-believing Christians without committing intellectual suicide in their various disciplines. Yet they would confess with every other Christian that there are many things they will not be told or understand until they finish their pilgrimage, and so they press forward.

But whether you are clever or not in human terms is not the point, for the Christian life is lived by the same principles whoever you are. Faith is not lived in a vacuum. It affects our way of life and directs our ambitions. Faith is for people who take their responsibilities in the present seriously, but who understand that there is something more than 'the now'. We can gain some idea of the practical implications of this from the experience of Abraham.

For Abraham, going to the Promised Land where God would lead him by definition meant leaving where he was living, not just physically but spiritually as well. For some of us it will probably be a spiritual journey, for I am not suggesting that we all have to literally uproot and go somewhere else. Abraham of course did not have the full 'gospel' understanding that has been given to us, but he was given clues. He was told that God is 'God Most High, Creator of heaven and earth' (Gen. 14:19). He is the one true God. Nevertheless Ur, where Abraham lived, was a place of idol worship. That was a fundamental reason why he had to leave.

We may not always know clearly where we are going, but we are certainly leaving behind what the New Testament describes as the 'world', for this world has many gods. As someone has said, 'Either our faith will separate us from the world or the world will separate us from our faith.' Even if that sounds a bit old-fashioned, it is undoubtedly true. Such a great God as ours and Abraham's, the one we know to be the Father of our Lord Jesus Christ, claims the pilgrim's worship, not idols of our own making.

There seems to be a clue as to what happens when idols claim our attention and allegiance – it could be home, career, family or possessions – in what happened to Abraham's father. Terah too set out on pilgrimage, but decided that Haran was quite far enough thank you. Now I am told that Ur to Haran is not very far, and not a very difficult journey either, seeing that they were both on the same side of the River Euphrates. Terah was not prepared to go far along the road to the promised inheritance because he was not prepared to lose his present one.

We have four daughters, and one of them had a delightful turn of phrase when she was small. On one occasion when she was about five or six she got into difficulties in a swimming pool at a church garden party. After she had been successfully fished out, my wife said to her, 'How awful that your feet did not reach the bottom.' 'Oh my feet reached the bottom,' she replied, 'but my head did not reach the top.' On another occasion she fell out of the bunk of a yacht while we were on holiday. While her mother was comforting her, my daughter diagnosed the problem like this, 'I got in too close to where I got out.' She made the point exactly as to why so many fail to keep going on the pilgrimage. Staying too close to where they begin, they do not go in or on far enough along the pilgrim way.

There is a marvellous book by Eugene Peterson called *A Long Obedience in the Same Direction*. It is a set of expositions for the Ascent Psalms and I recommend it to you. Its thesis is that when God's people went on pilgrimage to Jerusalem they kept going. There were many dangers along the way, ranging from wild beasts to bandits, but they kept going. They did not try to take short cuts across the mountains; they journeyed along the appointed path till they arrived in Jerusalem, the mountain of God.

Now I would hate you to imagine that there were no problems for Abraham along the road, for there were. Some of them were of his own making – especially when *twice* he made a complete fool of himself in Egypt. On another famous occasion God tested him to the absolute limits in regard to his son Isaac. Was he prepared to sacrifice the very life on which all the promises of God seemed to depend? Yet it is the testimony of the book of Hebrews that Abraham lived 'like a stranger in a foreign country', for 'he was looking forward to the city with foundations, whose architect and builder is God' (Heb. 11:8–10). He lived in tents so that he could keep on the move until God gave him something permanent.

Here was Abraham's secret: he just kept going one step at a time. A desire for what lay ahead meant that he did not want to get caught up too much by the present. There was something about this man for he was given a nickname – the Hebrew (Gen. 14:13). I am told that this means the 'man from the other side', which leads to the last question – the difficult one. How did he know when he had arrived? I rather suspect that he never knew, and that he spent all his life waiting and looking for something more.

And that is about it really. I have asked my wife to put on my gravestone, if I have one, and if it's true, 'He Died in the Faith'. Then, and only then, will I know I have arrived. I sometimes jokingly tell her to put 'He Died in the Faith – Almost', for there will be an element of surprise on my part. There is a wonderful old Methodist hymn that has this couplet

> May I then with *glad surprise*
> Chant thy praise beyond the skies.

My sentiments exactly.

'Pastor,' said my well-meaning church member, 'where is this church going?' Like Abraham, both corporately and individually we are not sure. It's not that we are odd or peculiar. It is not that God hasn't given us many things to enjoy now. We are not so heavenly minded as to be of no earthly use, but of this we can be certain: we are heavenward bound. When I was a little boy I was taken by special train with hundreds of others from Bristol to Harringay in London to hear Billy Graham. (I slept all the way through the service, but that is another story.) What I remember is the station ticket inspector saying, 'Platform number seven if you want to go to heaven.' Walking on and on one step at a time, enjoying much of the journey if we are blessed, and comforting and helping those who are less so, but constantly heading on till we arrive. Looking upward every day.

When the children were small we would pile them into the car to drive to Cornwall. Such was their almost blind faith, that they did not ask where they were going. They never asked where they would sleep, what they would eat, or even how long it would take. They trusted the driver, counted on the provision of their parents, and knew that with Mum and Dad all would be well. When they arrived, often in the middle of the night, there seemed no surprise, almost no realisation of the length of the journey, just the joy of being there. And I can promise you this, that when the pilgrimage is done, we will know for sure that we have arrived!

2

I'm confused about what God is doing: Habakkuk's story

When my wife and I were being taught to sail, we were taken to sea in a force eight gale (the rhyme is unintentional!) My wife found it terrifying, but I discovered an exhilaration that I had hardly ever known before. It was thrilling. On our return, I was crestfallen to be informed by our instructor that my greatest strength as a sailor was also my greatest weakness: I had no fear of the sea. Perhaps the greatest weakness that could ever befall anyone in the spiritual life would be to lose their fear of God. He is 'consuming fire', and even children are taught not to play with fire.

I presume that the majority of people who read this book are active Christians. Christians are by definition those who have had a past experience of the activity of God in their lives. They are ordinary people who have an expectation that God will have an active part to play in their future. They have been saved, and are trusting God to continue to save them whatever the future brings. Yet we are told that there are three tenses to salvation in the New Testament: we *have been* saved; we *will be* saved; we *are being* saved. Yesterday or tomorrow isn't really the problem, but today is. Some of us have a very shadowy idea as to what God is doing now. It is rather like Alice at her famous Mad Hatter's tea party, who was told that there was jam yesterday, there will be jam tomorrow, but no jam today. We have lost that expectation that God can break into our lives and use us now. It is the purpose of this chapter to try and ascertain why this should be.

Many of us cannot understand what God is up to – at this moment at least. Why does he allow things to happen that seem to injure me? Why does he not intervene and do something to help me at my point of need? It may be too extreme to call some of us 'walking civil wars', but it is not too extreme to say that we are 'walking question marks'! Why, why, why?

Once again we have someone who represents how we feel in the Old Testament. His name is Habakkuk. I would like you to read his short prophecy for it is one of the most powerful books in the Bible. It's easy to find – it's the book after Nahum! And if you did not find that very funny or helpful, look Habakkuk up in the index!

Habakkuk lived at rather a unique time in the history of Israel. He was ministering in about 600 BC at a time when there seemed to be an upturn in the spiritual life of Israel during the reigns of Josiah and Jehoiakim. If you are interested in this part of the history of Israel, you can read it up for yourself – it is a fascinating study.

Notwithstanding a degree of optimism in society, Habakkuk – like his contemporary Jeremiah – was a troubled man. He, like many of us, could not make out why God allowed certain things to happen. Why would God permit the Babylonians to enslave and destroy his promised people? It did not seem to make sense.

If you have read the book of Habakkuk, you at once discover that he is different from every other Old Testament prophet. In fact, he gives no message from God to Israel at all. Instead of saying 'Thus saith the Lord', he seems to be taken up with his lack of understanding of what God was about. In fact, rather than representing God to man, Habakkuk is the prophet who represents us to God. He asks our questions for us.

'How long, O LORD, must I call for help, but you do not listen?' 'Why do you make me look at injustice?' 'Why do you tolerate wrong?' and 'Why are you silent . . . ?' (Hab. 1:1–4, 13) are the questions he asks. Some 2,600 years later, many of us are still asking exactly the same questions. 'Why, God, have you let this happen to me? I can't understand what you are doing.'

Now I want you to accept a challenge. Read the first chapter of Habakkuk again, and then the last three verses of the book. Of course, that is not allowed when you are reading a novel, but this is not a novel. The change in Habakkuk's thinking is startling, and I want you to question how this incredible transformation in the prophet's thinking came about. What has happened to the man? For here, at the end of the third chapter, are some of the most sublime, trustful and mature verses in the Bible. William Cowper paraphrased them like this. It might sound a bit old-fashioned, but it is powerful none the less:

> Though Vine nor fig tree neither
> Their wonted fruit should bear,
> Though all the field should wither,

Nor flocks nor herds be there,
Yet, God the same abiding,
His praise shall tune my voice;
For, while in him confiding,
I cannot but rejoice.

So I repeat my question. How was Habakkuk brought from a place of complete confusion as to what God was doing, or not doing, to this place of quiet and absolute trust? Can we, in the darkest hour of the soul, have a similar experience? The secret must be hidden somewhere in what Habakkuk has written.

As I read his book I discover that Habakkuk had a deep understanding of the character of God. He describes him as 'O LORD' and 'O Rock' (Hab. 1:12), and even more than that he employs what is comparatively rare in the Old Testament: personal pronouns – '*My* God, *my* Holy One'. Not only does he have a big understanding of God, he also has a personal experience of him as well.

So let's get this clear: Habakkuk's questions about the activity of God are balanced by an inner understanding of who God is. When you know someone well, you can ask him or her the most direct of questions. A few years ago, my wife and I had the privilege of visiting Papua New Guinea. One of the disconcerting things there is that the people come up to you and ask how old you are – just like that. In our culture such a direct question would be considered rude, so you have to find out by other means! But Habakkuk is never rude with God.

When I was a young minister I attended a minister's fraternal where J. B. Phillips was present. People of my genera-tion will always be grateful for this man for he was the author of the first paraphrases of the New Testament. At that time there was so little available in modern English. Phillips once wrote a book called *Your God Is Too Small*. I sometimes wonder if, were he alive today, he would write another book entitled *Your God Is Too Cheap*. It is my contention that much of this generation of evangelicalism has grown just a little pally with the Almighty. Familiarity has tended to breed contempt. From the way that Habakkuk addresses God, you will see that they were never chummy.

In the nineteenth century, men who had an evangelical experience founded the Oxford Movement, which led to what we now know as the Anglo-Catholic wing of the Church of England. Some continued their journey right into the Church of Rome. One of these was Cardinal Newman, who was brought up in Ham, a district of Richmond, where much later we planted an evangelical church. Cardinal Newman had a great understanding of the transcendence of God. Speaking of the Almighty he wrote:

> In all his works most wonderful
> Most sure in all his ways.

In his heart of hearts, Habakkuk realised this too.

Another of these Anglo-Catholics wrote:

> My God how wonderful thou art
> Thy majesty how bright
> How beautiful thy mercy seat
> In depths of burning light.

Habakkuk may not have understood what God was about, but he never doubted the sovereignty of God. God is a being shrouded in mystery. If we understood him, he would not be God. The Bible describes his ways as being unsearchable and beyond our understanding, and he is not subject to our every whim.

Prayer is a complex matter and an area where I have personal difficulty. Undoubtedly one important aspect of prayer is telling God how it is with us, letting it all hang out, speaking as 'friend with friend'. Yes indeed. My children never made an appointment to talk with me. They did not dress up what they had to say in fancy Jacobean language. *Abba* means 'Father', we are rightly told. So Jesus taught us to pray 'Our Father', speaking of the imminence of God. But the Lord's Prayer continues with 'who art in heaven', and that speaks of God's otherness or transcendence. It is best if we take the name of God on our lips with extreme care.

So I would counsel against a casual, throwaway line such as 'God told me', or 'the Holy Spirit led me' unless you are quite sure that that is true. What if we were to say 'God told me' to establish our own position or to put our understanding beyond the realm of debate, so that it could not be tested? That would be very dangerous. I do believe that God speaks to us through his Word, that he reveals his way by his Spirit. God has led me over the years through reading and teaching Scripture, circumstance, the testimony of a friend, or an 'inward witness' corroborated by biblical norms of interpretation. But when well-intentioned people have come to my vestry and said, 'God has told me', and have then asked, 'But what do you think, Pastor?', it does put me in a hole, for what *I* think would hardly seem to be the issue! For all Habakkuk's questions, he never for a moment lost his awe of God. 'But the LORD is in his holy temple; let all the earth be silent before him' (Hab. 2:20).

When we have questions in our lives it is so easy to look for answers in the wrong places. We expect God to act in certain prescribed ways, usually in ways that please us. When I am physically well, surrounded by my family or in some beautiful place, then I can see the hand of God and praise him for his intervention in my life. And that of course is right, for all of those things are the goodness of God. But that was not the experience of Habakkuk, as we will see.

In response to his questions, Habakkuk is told by God to look and be amazed because he was going to do something so incredible that he would not believe it even if he were told (Hab. 1:5). Now that sounds pretty exciting. But rather than it being anything that Habakkuk could have hoped for or wanted, God was going to bring unutterable disaster upon the nation. 'I am raising up the Babylonians' (Hab. 1:6) says God, and that meant destruction, death and captivity. How strange the activity of God can be.

Nobody covets disaster. All of us would wish for a petal-strewn path to heaven. But that was not the experience of the people in the Bible. They found God when they cried, they met him in the storm as well as in the sunshine, not only in victory, but also in defeat. It is not just an Eastern proverb that says 'continual sunshine makes a desert', it is also scriptural for there is such reality in the Bible. The Psalmist is told that God is a refuge and strength *in* trouble. Paul is assured that God's grace is made perfect *in* weakness. The disciples were puzzled when they were at sea in a storm, while Jesus slept in the stern of the boat. Not only had he commanded them to be there, but by sleeping his attitude also seemed to indicate that he did not care. But there were lessons to learn in the storm that could not be learnt elsewhere. The 'peace be still' that the disciples heard that night on the lake of Galilee is still spoken by Jesus to those who are in the centre of the storm. The peace of God, which famously 'passes all understanding', is a peace that the world cannot give and that the world cannot take away. That truth is hardly new, but it could not be more important that we learn to understand it. To learn this lesson is to be preserved from being a fair-weather Christian.

When my children were young they would play at building castles with playing cards. Needless to say, I would blow them down when they were not looking! I was that sort of dad, I'm afraid. As far as I was concerned, their getting mad at me was all part of the fun. But when someone becomes angry with God at the first puff of wind, that is sad. 'Why has this happened to me?' is a recurring question I have been asked as a pastor. The truth of the matter is that, as a mere mortal, I have never had an adequate answer to that question. But if we move from a particular situation to general principles, there are some suggestions that can be made and they can be discovered in the experience of Habakkuk.

When Habakkuk is anxious to understand what God is saying to him, he does something about it, he tries to find out. He is a true prophet when he says, 'I will stand at my watch and station myself on the ramparts; I will look to see what he will say to me' (Hab. 2:1). Dare I suggest that this is the prophetic ministry that is needed today? We do not just need someone telling us that God loves us – true as that undoubtedly is and constantly worth saying. Instead, we need someone who is in a prominent place where they can see society today and ascertain something of what God has to say. Someone with the wider perspective, who can bring a word to this nation that is timely, relevant and brings the Word of God to bear upon it.

We, like Habakkuk, live in a time of spiritual declension.

The statistics reveal that institutional religion is in serious decline. Only a few years ago we could speak of retraction within the mainline churches, but console ourselves that evangelicals were bucking the trend. Today that is not true. I mentioned earlier that I have the great privilege of being chairman of the Evangelical Alliance, so I do have some idea of what is going on in the Church today. It is my contention that the spiritual tide is well out. I know that there are glorious exceptions, and I for one, along with Habakkuk, want to discover what God is saying. My fear is that in Britain today God is doing something that we neither expected or wanted: he is judging us. Like Israel of old, we have received so much from God in the way of spiritual leadership, historic revival, recovery of truth and the expectation of power in the Spirit. And what have we done with these great blessings and benefits? By and large, we have wasted them.

When I was a student in Scotland there was a very noisy young man in the study bedroom next to mine. The fervour of his personal devotions resonated not only through the wall, but also down the corridor. On enquiry I was told that the explanation for this ferocity in prayer was that he was a charismatic. To my knowledge, that was the first time I had heard the word in its modern theological sense. At that time, another movement of the Spirit in the recovery of the knowledge of the sovereignty of God was in full swing. It touched my life and affected my thinking. But that was a long time ago. Today, no section of the Church, whether 'reformed' or 'charismatic', can look at Britain today and claim that *it* was the agency that turned the nation of God. As in the day of Habakkuk, there is a spiritual dearth in high places, and God, I believe, is judging our nation. We have scriptural warrant for believing that. God's dealings with his people in the days of the prophets demonstrate this, and Scripture is a permanent record of the activity of God.

Habakkuk was the Word of God to his generation and he gave a rather amazing picture of inspiration. 'Write down the revelation and make it plain on tablets so that a herald may run with it. For the revelation awaits an appointed time' (Hab. 2:2–3). The message of God is written down, made permanent, made plain and understandable, brought to us by the messenger of God, and will become clear in time. God's unchanging Word, clearly understood, made plain by the Spirit of God and proclaimed by God's true messengers, will come to pass. The Babylonians did attack Jerusalem. God does judge his people.

Habakkuk knows that God's purposes will be known in history. He will conquer the forces of darkness. Another of the hidden verses of Habakkuk says, 'the earth will be filled with the knowledge of the glory of the LORD, as the waters cover the sea' (Hab. 2:14). And if we should imagine that somehow this worldwide rule counts me out, remember that nations are composed of individuals – and that means you and me.

There are other lessons that Habakkuk had to learn. Tucked away in chapter two is a verse that has changed the world more than once. He says, 'the righteous will live by his faith' (Hab. 2:4b). It was this verse that Paul used in Romans and Galatians to establish his great foundation doctrine of justification by faith. Paul declares that salvation is not achieved via something that *we* can *do*, but by faith in what God has done on the cross. It is not gained by us trying to impress God with our good works. Instead, it is brought about by our leaning on his grace; trusting in his love in sending Jesus to die on the cross in our place, to do for us what we could not do for ourselves by paying the price of our sin and washing it away by his blood.

Some 1,500 years after Paul there was a pious monk in Germany who desired peace with God more than anything else. He discovered that no self-mutilation of the body could bring about this peace. Being an academic, it was his responsibility to give a series of lectures on Galatians. Opening the Bible Martin Luther found Habakkuk's little verse (Gal. 3:11), and at a stroke he understood what had almost been forgotten: that the righteous live by faith.

Another couple of hundred years later there was to be found in Oxford a group of people who were so punctilious about their religion that they were called 'Method-ists'. One of them, John Wesley in fact, went to America as a missionary, but at that time knew little of the joy that comes from peace with God. I never cease to thrill at his conversion. On the evening of 24 May 1738, he was present at what sounds like a remarkably boring service in a Moravian Chapel in Aldersgate Street, London. (Near Bart's Hospital in the City of London if you want to make a pilgrimage.) Someone was reading from Martin Luther's preface to Paul's epistle to the Romans on justification by faith. What happened next I will tell in Wesley's own words:

About a quarter before nine, while he was describing the change which God works in the heart through faith in Christ, I felt my heart strangely warmed. I felt I did trust in Christ, Christ alone for my salvation. And an assurance was given me that he had taken away my sins, even mine, and saved me from the law of sin and death.

Once again Habakkuk 2:4b had changed history, for along

with others Wesley saw God at work in a revival so far-reaching that some called it an Evangelical Revolution. From this 'revolution' so much was to follow, including the modern missionary movement, social and political upheaval, the Evangelical Alliance, and so on.

And yet the emphasis in Habakkuk is slightly different. He is not talking about saving faith, but rather faith to live by. The New Testament definition of this sort of faith is very significant. 'Now faith is being sure of what we hope for and certain of what we do not see' (Heb. 11:1). And this brings us back to our context. What is the need for faith when God is always visible? Habakkuk developed a faith in God when everything else seemed to contradict the fact. Although he knew the dreaded Babylonians were coming, he could say with the hymn-writer:

> His love in time past forbids me to think
> He'll leave me at last in trouble to sink.

Chapter three of Habakkuk's 'prophecy' recounts in poetic form God's dealings with his people through their history, for God's people needed to be reminded of that. In much the same way, we are commanded to take communion 'in remembrance' of what Christ has done for us on the cross. 'Tell me the old, old story, for I forget so soon', I used to sing. Like you, I too have a personal history and wonder why I forget it so quickly. One moment's thought, though, and I am made aware of the many things that God has done for me. So many sins have been forgiven, so many needs have been met, so many disasters have somehow 'worked together' for good. It was this realisation that brought Habakkuk to his all-time high-water mark of personal trust.

When you remember how short Habakkuk's creed was compared with ours, and the fact that he had never even heard of the name of Jesus, there is not only something deeply moving about what he says, but something rebuking and challenging too:

> Though the fig-tree does not bud and there are no grapes on the vines, though the olive crop fails and the fields produce no food, though there are no sheep in the pen and no cattle in the stalls, yet I will rejoice in the LORD, I will be joyful in God my Saviour. The Sovereign LORD is my strength; he makes my feet like the feet of a deer, he enables me to go on the heights (Hab. 3:17–19).

Wonderful! Lord, please give me a faith that has the confidence to believe that as you have been in the past, so you will be in the future, so that I can look forward with the certain confidence that the Faithful One will be true to his word and promise.

The trouble for some of us is that we need to see and understand everything that God is doing now. The disciple Thomas was rather like that. He was an empiricist. In other words, unless he himself could touch the wounds of Christ, he could not believe that Jesus had risen from the dead. Jesus came to Thomas personally and said, 'Peace be with you!' (John 20:26). Then came an invitation to see and touch; eventually Thomas needed no more and cried, 'My Lord and my God!' (John 20:28). But there was still a gentle rebuke for Thomas when Jesus said, 'blessed are those who have not seen and yet have believed' (John 20:29). That must be the word of Christ to us. Don't insist on seeing and understanding everything – remember that the righteous live by faith.

Some years ago I was in Madras in India to speak at a student conference. The man who was driving me from the airport pointed to a hill and said, 'That is St Thomas' Hill.' 'Why?' I asked rather lamely. 'He preached the gospel there,' came the reply. The man could see that I was a little sceptical, but insisted that there is a strong tradition that St Thomas went to India and preached the gospel there. In fact, he assured me, considerable research had been done on the matter. Thomas could not recover the Upper Room experience, that was history, but its never fading reality drove him thousands of miles in the service of the master.

When we find ourselves in difficult, painful and confusing circumstances, we are in the same boat as the Church of all ages that stretches from before Habakkuk right up to the present day. A minister friend of mine told the following childish, yet effective, illustration on a church weekend. Brer Fox had caught Brer Rabbit as usual. This time it seemed serious, for the fox was swinging him round and round through the air by his feet. Seeing a brier patch, Brer Rabbit began to mutter, 'Oh no, not the brier patch, please not the brier patch.' Needless to say, Brer Fox hurtled the unfortunate rabbit straight into the brambles. Whereupon up popped the head of Brer Rabbit with the cry, 'Born and bred in a brier patch, born and bred in a brier patch.' That is the story of the Church of Christ and its individual members. They have triumphed in the prickliest of situations and have proved that the grace of God is sufficient in the most wretched of circumstances.

We are not told what happened to Habakkuk, but if he was alive when the judgement came it could not have been pleasant. But now, I think, rather than questioning the purposes of God, he had learnt to be quiet and trusting.

So if the judgements of God are inevitable, and the way ahead is going to be rough, does that not release me from all personal responsibility, or at least from the necessity of living the holy life? Not at all. It was Paul who asked the question, 'Shall we go on sinning, so that grace may increase?' (Rom. 6:1). The reason that some of us have lost that intimate sense of the presence of Christ is for that very reason. Isaiah said, 'Your iniquities have separated you from your God; your sins have hidden his face from you' (Isa. 59:2). Jesus said that it would be the pure in heart who would see God (Matt. 5:8).

Somehow Habakkuk inwardly knew that God was in control, despite the horror of what was going on outside. We too may not be able to avert God's judgement upon society in general, but we can still experience personal quietness of soul in the tempests of life – rather like the martyr Stephen, I suppose, who had the face of an angel even while the stones were raining down.

3

No one understands me:
Joseph's story

It is supposed to be just little girls who are made of 'sugar and spice and all things nice', but I am sceptical for there are some people of both sexes who are born 'nice' and without any of the above ingredients. Everyone likes them. They are popular, and apparently everything that they hope for falls into their laps. There are others who, whether through lack of personality, lack of communication skills, or inbred insensitivity, never seem to be recognised or appreciated. To be of the latter group can lead to an inferiority complex linked to a lack of self-worth. I have heard something like this expressed many times, 'If no one else likes me, then God doesn't either.' And another frequent response has been, 'No one understands me.'

I have to admit that I have never 'taken to' Joseph and have rarely preached about him. And that is the point, for people we do not like are often ignored. Of course, it is almost inevitable that we identify with some Bible characters more than others, and Joseph (like Elisha) for me falls into the non-identification group. I have often wondered why. There could be two explanations.

In one school of evangelical biblical interpretation Joseph is seen as a 'type' of Jesus Christ. The inevitable outworking of that is obvious, for to criticise Joseph seems to hint at criticising the Saviour. Now of course if Joseph had really been without sin, he *would* have been the Saviour – so we need not worry too much about that. So perhaps my reaction to Joseph is similar to my reaction when other people seem to go overboard about someone and make more of them than appears to be justified. In others words, perhaps I am a bit jealous.

But my real problem does not stem from a theological difficulty, but an emotional reaction. Joseph is so *nice*. As my sister used to say of the Josephs of this world, 'If they fell into a cesspit they would come up smelling of roses.' Joseph seems to have been a natural when it came to the 'good man' stakes. There seems hardly to have been a moral hiccup in his life. Undoubtedly, horrid things happen to him but he comes through them every time with no stain on his character. In fact, Joseph seems too good to be true.

Perhaps the reality is that he is so dissimilar to me that I can't understand what makes him tick. If that is the case, then I am not alone, for Joseph's own family could not understand him either. Lack of being understood must have been one of Joseph's greatest problems, and I expect he wondered why. The problem is that we can always see the faults in other people without understanding our own deficiencies. It was this sort of thing Jesus was talking about when he spoke of us seeing specks of sawdust in our brother's eye without realising that we have a plank of wood in our own. Incidentally, that is a very funny picture. When Jesus first used the illustration, there would have been roars of laughter from his listeners. Why is it that we never think of Jesus as having a sense of humour?

It is a horrid thing to feel that we operate on a different wavelength from anyone else: when — along with Joseph — our best intentions are unappreciated or, even worse, misunderstood. We strive for the best, but everyone else seems to find us a turn-off. We climb higher in positions of influence and power, but still feel vulnerable and alone. We feel God has given us a ministry, but no one else recognises it. If any of these feelings or similar ones are true for you, then Joseph is your man. But I should also warn you that he deserved some of the problems he faced, as perhaps we do too.

Yet Joseph also faced other problems for which he was not responsible, and they had a crippling, long-term effect. Joseph suffered from favouritism at home. A weakness in one generation can often be passed on to the next. In this case, the result was almost literally fatal. The hatred Joseph engendered by the partiality showered upon him by his father almost cost him his life.

The home situation was this. His father was comparatively old when Joseph was born. His mother Rachel was his father's first love, but not his only love, so Joseph's brothers were his half-brothers and much older than he was. With Joseph being the favourite, it was a home where trouble was brewing. We cannot totally blame Joseph if he grew up to be a crazy mixed-up kid.

But there was more. Genesis tells us that among Joseph's less endearing traits was a weakness for telling tales on his brothers. And to compound matters further his father fitted him out in special clothes. Now it does not take a professional to tell us that this boy is going to have problems. Please excuse the pun, but he was tailor-made for trouble.

This famous coat of many colours is the key to under-standing much of the cause of Joseph's problem. I am told that it would have been made from many pieces of cloth, each a different colour. It would have been a tunic with sleeves and was a garment synonymous with class and authority. If there was to be a modern comparison of this coat worn by Joseph and the clothes worn by his brothers, it would be something like this. Imagine a farming family where everyone wore jeans, while the youngest wandered about in a tailored, pinstripe suit. It was a mark of being different, of being freed from manual work. In reality, it indicated that Joseph was being marked out as the heir apparent of his father. Certainly, it did not make for close family relationships. Dressing up the lad in this sort of gear was wrong and inappropriate. Inevitably it caused trouble, trouble not directly of Joseph's making. It is not surprising that people had difficulty liking him or under-standing him. Or, what was more likely, they could not even be bothered to try.

Added to all this, Joseph had some traits of his own that complicated matters. He went in for dreams. And if that was not enough in a hard-working, down-to-earth sort of family, the dreams were about him. And to make matters *even* worse (if that were possible!), these dreams portrayed Joseph in such an exalted light as to make his brothers froth with rage. As they say, this is not the way to win friends and influence people. To the retort 'but the dreams proved to be true', I would reply that it might be true that I am the most handsome, intelligent and gifted man in the world, but it will not further people's regard for me by talking about it! It was neither wise nor appropriate for Joseph to speak to his brothers in the way that he did.

Perhaps what Joseph needed was a clip behind the ear or, as in the case of my daughters, being sent to their bedrooms. (Incidentally, I could never work out why this was such a dreadful – if not the ultimate – punishment for my children. Often, there was nothing that they enjoyed more than being in their bedrooms!) Yet the story of Joseph is given in the Bible for a purpose. We can neither wash our hands of him, nor try to condone and justify him. We can learn from him, though, for he is recorded in Scripture for our instruction.

As with Joseph, some of us are misunderstood because we deserve to be. We have a view of ourselves that others find difficult to assimilate, or a way of expressing ourselves that causes offence and misunderstanding. Along with Joseph, this can be caused in part by problems at home. To use an old-fashioned expression, we have been 'spoilt'. It might be caused by favouritism, by continually getting our own way (which is much the same thing), or being given more than is good for us. That such experiences leave their scars, especially in keeping and fostering relationships with others, is well documented. Unable to understand the reason ourselves, we wonder why people find it hard to get on with us. Try as we may, and often we try very hard, somehow we feel unloved and misunderstood.

For Joseph, the route to full acceptance was long and difficult, but eventually – as with his father, Jacob – it led to reconciliation with his family and, just as important, with himself. There came a day when, although he could demonstrate that the dreams had been truly prophetic of the future, he is reconciled to his family with not a hint of 'I told you so'. But it took a long time. These dreams had come true not because of anything great in Joseph himself. The ramifications of life knocked him into shape. Just as wind and rain can mould rock into different shapes, so the vicissitudes of life moulded this man into something that was wonderful. The disasters and triumphs of life were used to knock Joseph into the wonderful personality he clearly became. He could testify at the end that God had meant it for good – but at what a cost.

Sadly, in circumstances that were cruel and despicable Joseph was forced to leave home and fend for himself. His half-brothers decided to sell Joseph as a slave into Egypt. They made it appear to his father Jacob that he was dead, killed by some wild beast. There in Egypt, hundreds of miles from home, presumed dead, nobody's favourite except his father's – who was now beyond reach – Joseph had to start rebuilding his life alone.

There are two features of Joseph's personality that impress me greatly, and the first is his strength of character. I might not instinctively like the man, but he is marked by integrity. I have known people in my life that you might not want to go on holiday with, but they display characteristics that one can but admire. They keep their word, they are consistent, and they are true. I think I would rather have people like that around me than the big personality, the ready wit, and the enjoyable company – yet who are untrustworthy and inconsistent.

When Joseph, through no fault of his own, found himself in a morally compromising situation, he ran away. When he was languishing forgotten in prison for a crime he did not commit, there is no hint of bitterness. When he can serve his fellow prisoners, he does. When he has opportunity for revenge against his brothers, he does not take it. When there is opportunity for reconciliation that is proved genuine, he takes it with open arms. Perhaps, even if I am not yet instinctively liking the man, I am beginning to recognise and appreciate his qualities. After all, that is the way that Christians should approach everyone. We are not commanded to *like* everyone, but we are commanded to *love* them.

The other feature of Joseph that commends him to me is that he is someone with aspirations and longings. He is not so much a dreamer as a visionary. Certainly his visions (I use the word in a general sense) could have been more sensitively expressed, but that is the thing about longings and visions – they *are* so difficult to express. There was a dimension to Joseph that his family could not understand. They looked down and around while Joseph looked up. As a consequence, he was ridiculed, hated and rejected. People are suspicious when they find in another what they cannot recognise in themselves. Hopes and ambitions that they cannot share or experience for themselves offend them. To his brothers, Joseph is spoilt and has to be destroyed. To be different, with aspirations, is to be in danger both in society and often, sadly, in the Church.

A young person within the Church who 'gets above themselves' with their ideas, hopes and vision is treated with great caution. They might not be counted as mad, but after all, people reason, it's the pastor and deacons who are supposed to have the dreams round here. It is strange, is it not, that when young people qualify for their profession, get on and make money, we have no problem understanding that. In fact, we applaud them for it and are justifiably proud. But let the same person become really serious about spiritual things, or start saying things like, 'I believe that God wants me to . . .' or, 'I believe that the Lord is telling me that . . .' then manifest disease sets in. That's getting heavy, man.

Scripture says that where there is no vision the people perish. Joel, in a prophecy only partly fulfilled at Pentecost, said something very strange. 'And afterwards, I will pour out my Spirit on all people. Your sons and daughters will prophesy, your old men will dream dreams, your young men will see visions' (Joel 2:28). 'Not round here, they won't', says many a church leadership!

I don't think Joel was speaking of the pretty pictures and fanciful nothings that sometimes pass for visions today. He was saying that both young people and older people might, by the Spirit, see something of the divine programme for their own lives and the life of the Church and nation. That is how it was with Joseph. He could have worded it much better in the light of his audience – visionaries often can – but God had told him something of his plan for the future and it had to be passed on.

'Nobody understands me,' you say. Then let me ask you this question. What are your longings? What are your dreams? Would you be a better person if they came true? Would we be better Christians if they came true? Would the Church be stronger if they came true? Someone has said, 'If you tell me your dreams, I can tell you what you will achieve with your life.'

This is the world's verdict on Joseph's dreams: they are autosuggestion; he has a vivid imagination. But later we discover they are visions of faith and promises of God. Certainly the Church has the right, even the duty, to test vision to see if it is consistent with the revealed purposes of God. It is the leadership's responsibility to try and see whether there is any contradiction with the written word of God. But when someone says, 'The Lord has called me', then I discover in the Bible that God does call. When someone says, 'God has sent me', I discover that this is what God has always been doing – and so why not now?

William Carey told his Baptist ministerial colleagues in Northamptonshire that God had called him to preach the gospel in India. He was told to sit down! But, nothing daunted, to India he went under the auspices of the newly founded Baptist Missionary Society, thereby inaugurating the modern missionary movement. Gladys Aylward applied to the China Inland Missionary Society and was turned down. But to China she went and the rest is history. People with a dream may not always be received warmly, or be easy to know and work with, for they are often misunderstood. But, nothing daunted, they change things. Individuals, churches and even history are changed by their unswerving obedience to what they believe God has said and called them to do.

But it must all have been very confusing for Joseph. Instead of climbing high, he was put into a pit. Instead of being someone important, he was given a menial job, falsely accused, thrown into prison, and forgotten. I wonder how many times he asked 'Why?' 'What is God doing?' I think I can tell you. Jacob, his father, had been turning Joseph into a creep, but God was making him into a man. Through honest hard work, suffering and consistency, he was being prepared for his great calling. As much as any other, Joseph became a man who changed history.

'No one understands me for I am a dreamer.' Yes, but are you *only* a dreamer? Perhaps there comes to my vestry a young man or woman who feels a sense of call to some ministry or another. They are surprised when I don't do a war-dance and make them flavour of the month. They are hurt when I pray with them and send them away. But, after all, it might just be a dream. But if it is of God, they will soon be back. Perhaps God gives many a dream to test preparedness for obedience, and that is all he wants to know. As with Joseph, time will tell the story.

I used to dream that I would play cricket for England, but it was only a dream. But there came a day when in Spurgeon's College, being interviewed to be accepted for training to the Baptist ministry, I saw a picture hanging on the wall of the young, clean-shaven Spurgeon. With poised finger he is depicted pointing to the sky. The picture was prophetic of all that this mighty preacher was to achieve in future years as he pointed thousands to Christ. At that moment I had a dream that no one and nothing has taken away. Of course, I have not even been a shadow of Spurgeon, but I can still say with our friend the hymn-writer:

> Happy if with my latest breath
> I might but gasp his name.
> Preach him to all and cry in death,
> Behold, behold the Lamb.

None of this is an excuse for us to be like the young Joseph, priggish and difficult. Some of us are not liked because we do not deserve to be. Some Christians – even significant leaders – have never allowed the Spirit to heal their personalities of things that damage effectiveness and the ability to function as they should. As a result, they have been severely handicapped in service. But, in the final analysis, it is better to have the reward of faithfulness to God than human praise.

Through the mediation of a grateful fellow prisoner, Joseph is finally brought into the presence of Pharaoh, stands before him, and is commissioned to be his trusted servant. This is not just my 'preachy' bit, for it is important. Paul speaks of much the same in his letter to the Romans. He says that through faith we are justified, and are given peace with God through our Lord Jesus Christ. Through Jesus, he says, 'we have gained access by faith into this grace in which we now stand' (Rom. 5:1–2).

To stand before God through Jesus is to be at peace with him and at peace with myself. When I am accepted in Christ, then I can begin to accept myself. I suppose it does not matter too much if I am misunderstood by others, if I am accepted by him. This standing of which Paul speaks is to receive God's commission and authority to be about his business. Like Joseph before Pharaoh, I am given responsibility for initiative and service in the kingdom.

The story of Joseph has an incredible ending. Right at the close of Genesis we read of him in full reconciliation with his brothers. Joseph says to them, 'Don't be afraid. . . . You intended to harm me, but God intended it for good to accomplish what is now being done, the saving of many lives' (Gen. 50:19–20). The brat has changed. The prig has grown up. For here he displays grace, wisdom and maturity. Regardless of what anyone does to him, Joseph has at last learnt to understand himself and is at peace with the world. He became a person that God used.

4

No one has any confidence in me: David's story (part one)

In a commentary I read during the preparation of this chapter, I came across the following poem by Goethe. By all accounts, he had been searching everywhere for knowledge, but his search had been unsuccessful:

> This case was mine too when at leisure,
> What all the sages wrote I read,
> When with their small wits they would measure
> The wealth of worlds around us spread:
> I thought of Samuel then, when he
> Made Jesse's sons in row appear,
> And when the seven were counted, said
>   Are all thy children here?

You could imagine David out in the field with the sheep, shouting, 'No! What about me?' But then realising that with seven elder brothers – some of them just as presentable as the oldest, Eliab – no one was going to take much notice of David. I have no doubt that there are thousands of gifted Christian people (and every Christian is gifted) who have never had the opportunity to exercise that gift through lack of recognition and opportunity.

One of my most frequently used expressions, which I must have picked up somewhere, is 'I have not got all the gifts of the Holy Spirit, but neither have you, so I need you and you need me.' Very often that is not the impression given, for so many today lack not only any recognition for ministry but also, and even worse, any sense that they are needed for anything at all. The impression has been given that their sole function is to fill a seat at church. They come and go for years with never a thought from the leadership that they have something to add to the fellowship. What is more, because of little encouragement, they do not even enquire of themselves what their gifting might be. There is the metaphorical shrug followed by a droop of the shoulders that indicates resignation to uselessness.

Much of my time as a pastor was spent in thinking and praying as to the roles that a particular member of the church or congregation might fill. However diligently this was done, there were still many left who received no recognition at all. There were of course those who always volunteered – God bless them: that proportion of people, without whom the church could not function, who were willing to do almost anything. Others, such as musicians, were drafted into the worship group within days and some had such an obvious gift that they were pounced on in a moment. But there must have been many more wondering when they would be recognised for service, and whether there was anything to recognise anyway.

Frequently I try to remember how it was with me when I was young. How was any possible gifting to be recognised? It is difficult to have an accurate memory of the past. For reasons that I will elaborate on later in the book, reasons that resulted in academic failure, there were always, in my estimation, plenty of 'elder brothers' around – even if one was not actually called 'Eliab'.

My first two forays into public speaking were nearly my last. At a junior Christian Endeavour meeting there was, I discovered, a practice of chain prayer. We sat in a circle and prayed round. Inevitably and unavoidably, the prayer headed for me. What was I to pray for? To my utter dismay, I heard myself mumble, 'God bless lorry drivers.' I must explain that I neither had a 'burden' for lorry drivers at the time, nor since I am ashamed to say. In fact, the only time I have thought about lorry drivers since is when I have been stuck behind one on the motorway, and even then I am not praying for their blessing. The humiliation of that prayer circle still haunts me, and even today I am uneasy in public prayer. The first time I preached, in any formal sense, was at the Sunday afternoon Men's Bible Class. It was a hot day and the men settled down to sleep with a firm resolve, and who can blame them? That first sermon, unrecorded and unremembered by the sleeping few (except by me, for I still have the notes), almost brought a ministry to a close before it had begun.

If you read the story in 1 Samuel 16 there can only be sympathy for Samuel's instinct that Eliab was the man to be appointed king in succession to the disgraced Saul. When Jesse, David's father, is asked to produce his sons for inspection, Eliab is the obvious candidate for apparently he had all the qualities for the job. 'Surely he is the anointed one.' For a start, he is tall and good looking (still often considered to be excellent qualifications for ministry – if you will forgive the sour grapes). Yet God teaches Samuel a fundamental lesson. 'The LORD does not look at the things man looks at. Man looks at the outward appearance, but the LORD looks at the heart' (1 Sam. 16:7). But that of course is the rub, for we have precious else to look at. By definition, when it comes to people, we can only judge by appearances. So if it is only God who can look from the inside out, how are we to recognise the Lord's anointed?

I have on my computer a game of patience called Free Cell. It is a fascinating game, but very time-consuming (and I ought really to take it off my hard disc). However, when I have an intellectual problem or need a brain-wave, I play this game for it seems to get the wheels turning. I have just downloaded it now as I have been wrestling with this question as to how we, mere mortals, are to recognise God's man or woman for a particular task. But more than playing a computer game is needed, for such a task needs much fervent prayer. Tragically, when it comes to recognising God's man or woman for a particular ministry, we often get it wrong. Even after much prayer, CVs have been checked, interviews have taken place, holy platitudes about God's leading have been uttered, time often proves the person chosen to be a mistake. The new minister is soon as equally maligned as the previous one. The new elder, we discover, is dictatorial and unsympathetic to the feelings of others. The long-anticipated youth leader does not show those marks of wisdom in handling young people that are so essential. I know I am overstating things for the point of emphasis, but looking as we must from the 'outside in', recognising leadership and gifting is a risky business.

If the wrong one is chosen, it does not take a genius to work out that the right one has not been chosen, and that the one God did have in mind has been overlooked. This leads to heartache, disillusionment and despair. And for those who make the wrong choice, important work can be set back many years. As long as we weigh gifting on the scales of education, appearance, status or track record, there will always be the forgotten, sidelined ones who say 'no one takes any notice of me'. As with David out in the field, many of the Lord's anointed are not even included in the selection process – let alone set apart for ministry. So what is to be done about such a distressing and potentially volatile problem? Back to Free Cell, or is there another solution?

Quite clearly, we have little alternative but to make value-judgements about people. It would be stupid to claim otherwise. Whether it is a pastor or Sunday school teacher, vicar or youth leader, elder or someone to staff the crèche, decisions have to be made on the evidence that is available. Much the same could be said for finding a husband or wife for that matter. Yet 'we felt led' or 'I thought I loved him' can both sound a little lame with the hindsight of experience.

A logical extension to our thinking that comes from being overlooked and unrecognised by others is to imagine that we are not in the mind of God. But that is something that we are never allowed to say, for the one who takes constant notice of us is God. He makes continual judgements upon our actions, thoughts and motives. The apostle John in his 'Revelations' says, 'And I saw the dead, great and small, standing before the throne, and books were opened. Another book was opened, which is the book of life. The dead were judged according to what they had done as recorded in the books' (Rev. 20:12). If you are a biblical Christian you will take that seriously. I do not mention this to increase the burden of the one who says, 'But I am never asked to do anything.' All of us long for God to say to us, 'Well done, good and faithful servant' – if only we had an opportunity to be a servant in the first place.

So it's hopeless then both for the ones with the responsibility for choosing, and the ones who vainly wait to be asked, for we make our choices from outward observation and get it all wrong. Well, it's not quite hopeless, for there are some aspects of a person's demeanour that point to the heart. The heart is the seat of our emotions in biblical thought, the place where our true self is to be found. The qualities that God is looking for are nothing to do with being gregarious, wealthy, articulate or influential, but something radically different.

It is a fascinating study to see what the qualities were in the disciples that Jesus recognised when he called them to follow him. There was nothing much to show on the outside, but we get it wrong when we imagine that the disciples were uncouth, uneducated and lacking in human qualities of leadership. Jesus knew what they would become. Some of them, in the hands of Christ, were able to lead churches, preach to thousands, turn the world upside down, as well as to write Gospels in very good Greek! Whatever the outward appearance, their potential must have been obvious to Christ. When Jesus called the Twelve they were ordinary, working folk. It was not so much what they were, but what they *became* through the call of Christ and the power of the Spirit. As with us, the potential of the disciples was staggering.

But initially that is all it was – potential – for sadly the disciples shared a negative quality. What they had in common was failure. We would never have chosen them for anything but a running-away contest. Nevertheless, it was to Peter, the arch betrayer, that Jesus asked, 'Do you love me?' And when the reply was in the hesitant affirmative, Jesus said to him,

'Feed my lambs' (John 21:15). It was to the disciples collect-
ively that Jesus said in effect, 'All authority is mine therefore
go and make disciples' (Matt. 28:18–19). It was of the 'chief of
sinners', Paul, the one who consented to the death of Stephen,
that the Lord said, 'This man is my chosen instrument to
carry my name' (Acts 9:15). And so we could go on. God
recognises and calls people whom we would reject as unsuitable. Jesus takes hold of disparate people united by their
inadequacies and makes them great in his service. Those we
would never recognise for high office, because apparently they
have so few of the qualities needed, are the ones he calls. For
reasons known only to him, he puts his treasure into earthen
vessels.

So does that mean we have to resign ourselves to non-
recognition and uselessness? Perhaps it does, for sadly that has
been the lot of many. Their face did not fit, they did not have
the right formal qualifications, or their 'gifting' was not
apparently in the area of the need and opportunity. But it
should not be like that, for it leads to wasted lives and bitter
spirits.

As something of an historian, I am interested in statues.
Walk around central London and look at the mighty people
depicted there in stone and bronze. There are kings and
queens, prime ministers, politicians and generals – particularly
generals and men of war. What is strange is that not many
healers, carers, people of peace and goodwill are remembered
in stone. Not many people who carry the attributes of Christ
have been lauded by society. They have not been recognised.
So why is it that some of the qualities that seem most
recognised by the world are also the most recognised qualities
in the Church, and those least regarded in the world are also
those least regarded in the community that bears the name

and attributes of Jesus? Why is it the strong and domineering, the manipulative and contentious, are often in recognised leadership, while the humble and meek are left unrecognised? 'Not by might, nor by power but by my Spirit', says the Lord, and this is a gospel principle. That is why he elects the insignificant to his service if we will but realise it. Of course, I remember the reason now – it is so that the glory will go to him.

There is a confirmation of this in the call of David. We can see a hint and a truth contained in the story of the recognition of David for kingship that needs to be highlighted. It demonstrates that our ways are not God's ways, and should be a guide to our understanding of who God is calling to work for him. First, a hint in the story (which I am sure is something more than preachers' licence or ingenuity, although it will turn into a sermon if I am not careful!). The Bible says that while the 'talent parade' was passing before Samuel, David was in the field tending the sheep. So what? Several things can be suggested from this for the encouragement of anyone who feels unrecognised but wants to be used by God.

Clearly, David was a young man who could take responsibility. It was no mean thing to be responsible for your father's livestock, but his father knew he could be trusted. A person who cannot be trusted to fulfil secular responsibility should never be recognised to exercise spiritual responsibility, which is far more important. Never imagine for a moment that because you have not been a success in the secular, that you will have a crack at doing something in the religious. Working for Christ is no easy option. It is true that Christ does take 'failures', but in the kingdom only our best will do.

We discover from the testimony of David that being a shepherd was a dangerous occupation. David saved his sheep from a lion and a bear. He made sacrifices, put himself in danger for the sheep. A person who, from a sense of responsibility, will do that for dumb animals can be trusted to look after people. And that is what ministry is about. It is about people, people whom God loves and Christ died for. It is being cared for, loved and supported by those delegated to this high responsibility, often at great personal cost.

David learnt many lessons from his shepherding career that stood him in good stead for the rest of his life – in fact, his secular life enhanced his kingship and coloured everything that he tried to do for God. David's life as a shepherd seems to have crept into David's very psyche. He incorporated looking after sheep into his Psalms. He spoke of the Lord being like a shepherd, for God was like one who leads his sheep beside still waters and green pastures. In other words, secular life became a training ground for future ministry and a constant source of insight. The lessons he learnt in the fields with the sheep, he applied to his calling as king. David had lived in the real world and proved himself there. He could be trusted with greater things.

The analogy of the Lord's servant being a shepherd permeates the whole of Scripture. The lessons David learnt stretch through the psalms, the prophecies of the Suffering Servant, to Jesus the Good Shepherd of John's Gospel and beyond. The Good Shepherd knows his sheep by name, he protects them, and when one is lost – even though ninety-nine are safe in the fold – he goes out and looks for it. David knew all about the duties of a shepherd before they had religious significance for him. The one who is recognised by God is the one who cares for the sheep.

In all my churches it is the carers and encouragers who have been the salt of the earth. What they did may not have had a fancy name, but when there was a need they were there. When someone was wanted to provide transport, they did it. When there was a hospital visit to make, they were there. When there was a word of encouragement to give, they gave it. Well, that all sounds very ordinary, you might say, but I suppose being a shepherd has been pretty ordinary in any age.

One of the signs of the immaturity of modern evangelicals is the Gadarene rush in search of the novel and extraordinary. I most firmly believe that the gifts of the Spirit are for today, but that does not help me to understand why it is only the exciting and dramatic that claim the attention of people. Imagine the great rally reaching its climax. The persuasive leader at the front says, 'While all heads are bowed and all eyes shut, I want those who desire the gift of encouragement to put up their hands.' The gift of encouragement is listed but, as with the gift of administration (which I do not have), it does not sound very interesting. But encouragement is of vital importance, and no Christian leader could survive without it. That is why 'people persons' are so often called by God, for they are like shepherds with the sheep, found among the sheep, feeding, caring and protecting the flock.

Now we come to the truth that I referred to just now. To begin with, I want you to use your imagination as Samuel asks for David to be brought to him and recognises him as the future king. 'You are going to be king,' says Samuel. 'That's nice,' says David – or words to that effect. 'So what do I do now? How do you play kings?' You see, David needed so much more than recognition. He had to be given the power to accomplish his calling. For David this came when he was anointed with oil. The Bible says that after anointing with oil 'the Spirit of the LORD came upon David in power' (1 Sam.

16:13). Having been recognised and set apart he was given the authority, wisdom and leadership skills that were essential to be a king. This verse is of more importance than might at first be recognised, for it tells how we too are empowered for service. Let me explain why.

My friend R. T. Kendall and I talk a great deal about 'unction'. To put it in another and less sanctimonious way, we long for power in our ministry. We know that unless God helps us by his Holy Spirit we will never achieve anything of lasting value for him. Now let me explain why this verse about David is of central importance to that longing for power. But I must warn you, we are now straying into the area of theology!

If the verse I quoted above, 1 Samuel 16:13, is a relevant Old Testament verse, its New Testament parallel is to be found in 1 John 2:20–7 where John is talking about power not for kingship, but power to know the truth. The word 'blessing' there can be translated 'unction'. This word 'unction' or 'blessing' is translated from the Greek word *chrisma*. Now before you start getting excited, that is not the same word as *charismata* – although of course they are related. But you will start getting excited when I explain to you that the Hebrew word for *chrisma* is 'messiah'. And 'messiah' is related to the Old Testament practice of anointing with oil – which is, of course, where David comes in.

Before 'messiah' had anything to do with people, it began with consecrating *things* used in the temple for service to God. But soon it became identified with *people*, setting them aside for the Lord's work by anointing with oil. Gradually the 'anointing' became linked with the coming of the Holy Spirit, as with David. He was recognised for ministry, set apart, anointed with oil, and then the Holy Spirit came down on him in power. Gradually the 'anointed one' became a title for the promised one who was to come: the Messiah himself. The Greek for Messiah is *Christos*. Christ is the Anointed One, the promised Messiah. In the Gospels we read that when Jesus was baptised, 'the Holy Spirit descended on him like a dove'. And what was the promise of Jesus to his disciples? 'John baptised with water, but in a few days you will be baptised with the Holy Spirit' (Acts 1:5). This promise was fulfilled on the day of Pentecost. And what of those who received the Holy Spirit? We are told that at Antioch the disciples were first called 'Christians', which means the followers of the 'Anointed One', or it can be translated as 'the anointed ones' – in other words, those who had received the Holy Spirit. So John says to his readers, 'You have received an anointing', an unction. You have been consecrated to a ministry, anointed and empowered by the Holy Spirit to know the truth.

Please forgive all this theology, but it is of vital importance (as theology usually is). It is not merely the assessment of what we are that is the issue, but of what we might become through the empowering of the Holy Spirit. It is not a call without the power to carry it out, but a promise that the Holy Spirit himself will give to us everything that we need. We look to ourselves and say no one takes any notice of me *as I am*. But Scripture says, 'It does not yet appear what we shall be', and that need not only refer to heaven. Indeed, we are 'being changed from one degree of glory to another'. 'Jesus you are changing me', we sometimes sing. When we are set aside for ministry, dedicated to some task for Christ, the Holy Spirit gives us power to carry it out. We become something more than we could ever have imagined. And that is not for something upfront, or humanly significant; it is for anything and everything that God wants us to do and become.

In the Introduction, I mentioned that when I was a student at Spurgeon's College I used to look at my year-group and think that none of us were cut out to be ministers. None of us will achieve anything, I thought. But I was forgetting the unction of the Holy Spirit. Having been recognised and consecrated for ministry, power from the outside was made available. And that is true for any service to which God calls us, however lofty or insignificant we imagine it to be.

To illustrate the point, let me quote from a dusty old commentary by J. P. Lange:

> Johann Tauler had preached many a learned sermon when Nicolaus of Basle, the Waldasian, visited and told him, 'You are a kind hearted man and a great minister, but you have not yet tasted in truth the sweetness of the Holy Spirit.' From that time on Tauler sought the true Teacher in Scripture and the cross, who teaches us more in one hour than all the earthly teachers can teach us to the last day.

That is what unction does.

Even after he was anointed king, kingship – that is, the power to be king or the recognition that being king demands – did not came to David at once. One Prime Minister (compassion demands that I do not mention his name) said that he could deal with inflation 'at a stroke'. He was wrong of course, for it took decades to bring inflation under control. David had to grow and develop into his new calling. It took some time, for it usually does. In 1 Samuel 17, during a battle against the Philistines, David is instructed to carry food to his brothers at the front line. He was still prepared to carry out a menial task, for anyone called of God will be prepared to do that. Seeing the scene with the opposing armies stretched across either side of the valley, aghast that a mere Goliath should reek such fear and despondency, David voices his defiance. At David's brave words against the enemy, Eliab, his eldest brother, says in effect, 'Who on earth do you think you are?' When Saul hears of it, the discredited king said much the same, 'You are only a boy.' Even the 'anointing' did not mean that David was at once given recognition of his high calling. He had to be patient.

David's first great victory was accomplished in a way that was unique to him. It was not in the armour of another, for this battle had to be fought in his way. The sling must have seemed an unlikely weapon, but David had perfected its use while looking after the sheep. No one else could do what he alone could do in the defeat of Goliath. The defeat of Goliath was absolute, the enemy routed, but for David it was only a beginning for so much that was to follow. God still had yet greater things for him. To become David the Psalmist would take some time.

'No one takes any notice of me,' we say. But if David is anything to go by, to be noticed by God is to be faithful where we are, responsible for the tasks we all have to do. To be like David with the sheep, we are to be trusted with small tasks so that we might become trusted with greater tasks. There are hundreds of things that we can do for God without having to receive the attention of others. Why do we want that attention anyway? Because we are human, I suppose. Yet step by step we can grow into the work God has called us to do until our calling is obvious to everyone.

When David is finally recognised as king by the people, they say something rather wonderful and prophetic about him. Let me quote it in full: 'We are your own flesh and blood. In the past, while Saul was king over us, you were the one who led Israel on their military campaigns. And the LORD said to you, "You shall shepherd my people Israel, and you shall become their ruler" ' (2 Sam. 5:2). All that insignificant shepherding, all those years of hard work for no recognition, had come to fruition. And in flowering into leadership, David never ceased to be one in flesh and blood with the people, for he never forgot how God used his past, investing it for his future ministry.

The frequency with which this model is seen in Scripture, particularly in Christ himself, 'that great shepherd of the sheep', suggests that this is more than a metaphor but a principle. For Christ there were thirty years of preparation; thirty years before John the Baptist said, 'Behold the Lamb of God.' The crowd – he describes them as his brothers and sisters, you will remember – were like sheep without a shepherd. The ministry was painful, the recognition minimal, the end terrible, and the obedience absolute. 'Therefore God highly exalted him.' That is something of the way we might have to travel before ultimate recognition and reward is given to us.

Martin Luther's schoolmaster used to shake each pupil by the hand every evening before they went home. When asked why, he said that he did not know what any of them might become. History confirms that he had a point – as might your history and mine.

5

I am not very gifted: Moses' story

False modesty gets up everyone's nose. You know the sort of person who says, 'Oh no, not *me*, dear', when in fact they are itching to be asked. Ugh!

It is strange, so strange that I can hardly believe it is true, that Moses, the great prophet of the first covenant, and Paul, the great apostle of the second covenant, were both ineffective as speakers. Surely, although both plead their lack of oratory skills, they must be exaggerating. This is the very sort of humility that we find grating. 'Ah, go on,' we want to say.

With regard to Moses there *could* be a debate as to both the motivation and the veracity of his statement to God, 'I have never been eloquent . . . I am slow of speech and tongue' (Exod. 4:10). It could be that it was simply an excuse, a desperate effort to get out of fulfilling the call of God that he knew would be both dangerous and costly in the extreme. 'Listen, God, you have got the wrong man because I am no speaker.' We could imagine saying it ourselves.

Or it could be that Moses is asserting an honest yet mistaken understanding of his own gifting. He honestly thought that through lack of a persuasive tongue he could never persuade Pharaoh to release the people or lead them on one of the great migrations of history.

Whether Moses was being genuine or not, Stephen (much later obviously) reports the accepted understanding of Moses' gifting when he describes him as 'powerful in speech and action' (Acts 7:22). So either Moses could not speak and God enabled him, giving him the gifting that he lacked, or it was an understandable yet flimsy excuse by Moses to get out of his calling. Assuming Stephen was right – that Moses did become a mighty speaker – God obviously equipped Moses in a way that had not been true previously. Whatever the reason for Moses' understanding of himself, and it may be a combination of reasons, there is great encouragement here for us because Moses' God is also our God. In time, God enabled Moses to overcome his fears and doubts and equipped him for service.

As for Paul, he too was adamant that he was not a natural speaker, and the cumulative evidence means that we have to believe him. No one could doubt that he was one of the greatest intellects of any age, that he was a supreme writer under the power of the Holy Spirit. The problem seemed to be either in his appearance or manner of speaking. 'His letters are weighty and forceful, but in person he is unimpressive and his speaking amounts to nothing' (2 Cor. 10:10) said his critics. ' "Timid" when face to face with you, but "bold" when away!' said these same sceptics of the apostle (2 Cor. 10:1). When Paul was on his feet and speaking, no one seemed very impressed.

That there is a gift of speaking is obvious. I know one

modern evangelical leader, whom I will not name, who could read the London telephone directory and make it sound riveting. Somehow he makes the most trivial things sound interesting. But there is another I know who writes like an angel, but when trying to bring home the same material in person – well, that is another matter! I suppose most of us are somewhere in between the two extremes.

Now clearly the ability to speak, when sanctified, is a great gift, and not to be deprecated. But even for an overt preaching or teaching ministry, it is not an essential gift. Moses and Paul prove it. Certainly history tells us that some of the people God most used in changing the spiritual climate of their day were mighty in the pulpit. Martin Luther, John Knox, George Whitefield, John Wesley and C. H. Spurgeon come immediately to mind. But with deep respect there are not many such among us today reading this book – or writing it for that matter! God in his mercy uses lesser material for his purposes. Perhaps it is better that way, for otherwise we would take a wrong view of ourselves rather than being dependent on the Holy Spirit to help and enable us.

Added to this, it seems to me that the secular world has become suspicious of oratory in itself. Lloyd-George, the Prime Minister at the time of the First World War, was renowned as a speaker, one who could attract and move thousands, but his style is now treated with suspicion and it would be folly to try to reproduce it. In fact, trying to replicate anyone is the height of stupidity. God called Moses and Paul because it was *them* that he wanted to use – as they were, as he could make them, not to be a pseudo someone else.

Several years ago I had the responsibility of being chairman of counselling and follow-up when Mission England came to East Anglia. I had the privilege each night of sitting immediately behind Billy Graham as he preached. With all due respect, and it has been said by others, it was not Billy Graham's oratory that brought people to the point of decision (including one of my daughters); it was God by his Spirit. That was the only explanation. To imagine I could return to my church and duplicate the same result by trying to initiate the same style and method would have been madness. There is only one Billy Graham, only one Robert Amess (forgive me for placing them together in the same sentence), and only one you.

Whether we like it or not, it is a life that speaks louder and more effectively than a voice, and what is achieved is of far more importance than the splendour and eloquence of the presentation. In effect, Paul says to the Corinthians that it is not him that matters, for 'You yourselves are our letter . . . known and read by everybody' (2 Cor. 3:2). The true verdict on the most eloquent sermon is the difference it makes in the hearts and lives of the hearers. The day seems to be gone when people would travel miles to hear a particular preacher. The princes of the pulpit seem to be dead, and perhaps it is better that way.

But let's get back to Moses. Was he serious? Was it just a cop-out – an excuse not to undertake what was going to be a costly calling? And what, in this context of being a speaker, is his relevance to us?

At the time of his conversation with God, Moses had recently had an amazing experience of him. He had met God in the burning bush and, more than that, God had revealed his name to him and had called him into his service (Exod. 3). The power of God had been demonstrated in his life by miracle and promise. Perhaps best of all, God had said, 'I will be with you' (Exod. 3:12). Yet despite all this, Moses doubted

God's calling on his life. To us, the protestation 'I cannot speak' sounds lame and unworthy.

Yet I remind myself, as I trust you will too if you are a Christian, that we have met God in Christ. He has called us individually and revealed himself by the names of Saviour and Friend. I have seen indications of the power of God in my life and have lived on the strength of his promises. But when the call to service comes and I say, 'But I can't because . . .' I seem to forget what I have known all along: that without God's help and empowering by his Holy Spirit, there is nothing I can do for him anyway in my own strength.

God's promise of help was at the point of Moses' individual need. 'But I cannot speak,' he says. 'I will help you to speak,' says the Lord. In fact, more than that, God did not only promise Moses that he would help him to speak, but that he would also teach him what he had to say (Exod. 4:12). Who could ask for more than that? Instead of Moses bringing out the one major problem – his lack of speaking ability – he should have remembered all that God had already done for him in terms of self-revelation. It is hardly surprising that God was angry with Moses (Exod. 4:14). To have God angry with us is serious, and sadly there would come a day when Moses would regret this altercation with the Almighty.

But even as I criticise Moses, I want to spring to his defence. Perhaps it was not that Moses lacked gifting but, as I've suggested before, he lacked confidence in being able to meet the demands that God was placing upon him. After all, it is no small thing to release a people from captivity and lead them to the Promised Land. That is not an everyday sort of commission for anyone! I am not surprised that Moses did not trust himself to be sufficient for the task, and surely humility is a commendable attribute. Yes it is, but within limits. Jesus says blessed are the poor and meek (Matt. 5:3, 5), and to his credit Moses was known as a meek man (Num. 12:3). But listen, Moses, someone has to fulfil the Lord's commission, and if it is not you, then it will be someone less qualified for the task.

What a tragedy if any of us were to waste a life and refuse a calling out of a false modesty or a fake humility. People like Charles Dickens's Uriah Heap are 'ever so 'umble', but they are a pretty slimy sort of person, of no use either to God or humanity. All of us are important to God, or otherwise he would not have brought us to himself. We were saved because, for some reason known only to him, God loves saving people. And secondly, we were saved for a purpose known to him and in time revealed to us. We are pretty important people. I remember the deaconess in my last church reminding a girl who, despite crippling difficulties, became great for God: 'You are a daughter of the king,' she told her. In other words, if we are in Christ then our potential is staggering.

I repeat, don't be impressed by Moses asking God to 'please send someone else'. A false humility, an ungodly self-distrust, gets up everyone's nose. In fact, Scripture condemns it. True, Paul tells the Romans, 'Do not think of yourself more highly than you ought, but rather think of yourself with sober judgment, in accordance with the measure of faith God has given you' (Rom. 12:3). God will not tolerate pride, but thinking of ourselves with 'sober judgement' means being realistic about ourselves and always remembering that those whom God calls he also equips. (I wonder how many times I have said that, and where I got it from?) Paul describes 'false humility' as the product of 'an unspiritual mind', a mind that is puffed up with unspiritual notions (Col. 2:18). False humility is an inverted pride and is therefore a sin. Each one of us is called to take a true view of capacity, gifting and ourselves. And one thing we must never do, for this too is a sin, is to deny or deprecate the grace of God in our lives.

There used to be a stupid sentimental song in vogue when I was young which had the line 'then my living will not be in vain', or something about 'never passing this way again'. Unfortunately, sentimental or not, it happens to be true. We only live once. This is the only life you will ever have and it would be the ultimate tragedy to waste it by a false humility. Habakkuk said that God enabled him 'to go on the heights' (Hab. 3:19), and that is what God does for even the most unlikely. To be kept back from the high places of the purpose of God for our lives could be his way of punishing us for disobeying his call to service – just being ordinary when God meant us to be great.

Sadly, Moses could not believe the promise of God. When God said to him, 'I will help you speak and will teach you what to say' (Exod. 4:12), that should have been enough for him. But tragically it wasn't, and his brother Aaron proved to be a very mixed blessing. God knows the one he is calling and what he can do to equip that person for the task envisaged. In fact, the lack of natural gifting could even be an advantage. Knowing that we are lost, other than by the intervention of God, drives us to prayer, causes us to rely on the Holy Spirit, and rouses us to effort.

I don't want to start another argument about Paul's thorn in the flesh, but it could just be that his lack of preaching and oratory gifts were the matters that he prayed three times should be removed (2 Cor. 12:7–10). Just a little earlier he had written rather poignantly, 'I may not be a trained speaker but I do have knowledge' (2 Cor. 11:6). Can you hear the pathos and defensiveness in those words? Paul feels his lack very keenly. In his first letter to the Corinthians he had said something similar: 'When I came to you, brothers, I did not come with eloquence or superior wisdom' (1 Cor. 2:1). It begs the question, 'Has this man a depressed obsession about his speaking gifts or was it true?' If the latter, which I most firmly believe, then God made him an overcomer and made him more sufficient than even Paul could fully accept. What he did accept was that God's grace was sufficient for him (2 Cor. 12:9).

The reason for all of this Paul gives us himself. Very movingly he says, 'My message and my preaching were not with wise and persuasive words, but with a demonstration of the Spirit's power, so that your faith might not rest on men's wisdom, but on God's power' (1 Cor. 2:4–5). Perhaps when we rely on natural gifting, the glory goes to us and that is disastrous. It is not that we have heard a great preacher or teacher that counts, but that we have heard God through that person.

Lips touched by divine grace have a natural gifting of their own. I have on many occasions heard simple Cornish Methodist lay-preachers demonstrate more unction, and reveal more of Christ to me, than many a trained preacher. The reason is that God was with them, and unless he had been, they of themselves would have had nothing to say.

If it came to the crunch I would rather have someone who spoke sincerely on my behalf, than a trained orator who took pleasure in words only for their beauty and cadence rather than what they could do for me. One of my sons–in–law is a barrister. If he were defending me, and I hope he will never be put into that situation, I would say, 'Steve, say it as it is. None of the professional stuff please.' Robert Hall, a Baptist divine of a previous generation, said:

> If I were put on trial for my life, and my advocate should
> amuse the jury with tropes and figures, or bury his
> arguments beneath a profusion of flowers of his rhetoric,
> I would say to him, 'Tut, man, you care more for your
> vanity than for my hanging. Put yourself in my place –
> speak in view of the gallows – and you will tell your
> story more plainly and earnestly.'

Quite so! That demonstrates that Robert Hall had a better
turn of phrase than I have, but it also underlines the truth that
some of the things we have to say are so important that they
are best told simply and with integrity of life and lip. Rather
than depending on a natural gift that enables the speaker to
say the right thing in a way that impresses the hearer's ear, but
never achieves anything, it is speaking from the heart that will
count.

Jesus promised his disciples that when the crunch came
they 'will be given what to say' (Matt. 10:19). If Moses had
trusted God, then with necessity his gift would have grown.
The provision of Aaron meant that Moses did not develop
the gift God would have provided. The message was diluted
of power by being delivered through an intermediary. Aaron
did what Moses would never have done, and what we should
never do. He took to himself what belonged to God and used
his influence and speech gifting in a way that was disastrous.
In the wretched story of the golden calf we have this telling
phrase, 'Aaron . . . announced' (Exod. 32:5). He used his
oratory in a way that was contrary not only to the revelation
of God in his law, but in a way that was to bring death upon
the people.

People who rely only on natural gifting have to be very
careful, for they have caused untold harm by their ability to

move people with rhetoric. We have seen it all too often in history, both secular and sacred, from the massed Nazi rallies of Munich to the mass suicides of extremist cults. Even rational men and women can be moved to destruction by mere words.

Now please don't misunderstand me. I am not decrying natural gifting, or the need for training and practice in its development. All I am saying is that the naturally gifted are in danger of becoming complacent, knowing that their talent will get them through. We have seen it all too often, when some preachers and teachers, without any preparation, manage to impress by stringing a few sentences together. For those not so gifted, where every word has been carefully prepared, where there is total dependence upon God to achieve anything, then the glory for any benefit goes to him.

For reasons I will not go into now, I had a lousy basic education. In fact, I left school with no qualifications at all – not even one GCSE or an O-Level. When I felt that God was calling me into the ministry, I had no understanding that I was 'gifted' or any expectation that I could be. I think my family and friends of that time would agree. But God stepped in and spoke to me through his Word and through trusted friends in a way that I could not deny. Try as I might, there is no better way of saying it. I felt 'called' to the ordained ministry. I have been a minister for thirty years, and it has not always been easy. My lack of basic education sometimes reveals itself in most intimidating ways. Although I can hear at once in others when there is a mistake in the 'I' and 'me', or 'who' and 'whom' syndromes, it does not come naturally when I myself am preaching. Sometimes my sermons have come to a complete halt as I have tried to work out in my mind some complex point of syntax. Believe me, that hardly adds to the flow of a sermon!

And nothing has changed over the years, but strangely being the minister of a highly articulate congregation has helped. When I have ground to a halt and said, 'Is it "I" or "me"?' we have laughed together and then I have carried on. That is what a minister resting on the love and support of his people can do. O that there were more congregations that would exercise the God-given grace of raising the confidence of their minister!

In one of my churches, a member of the congregation would come to the door after morning worship and say, 'Two split infinitives this morning, Pastor!' Yet I grew to love that man for other things. One of the supervisors of my MPh wrote to me to say that there was a hanging participle on page thirty-seven of my thesis! My wife and I had to peep into an English grammar book at W.H. Smith to discover what a hanging participle was. We discovered it had something to do with a word ending in 'ing', so we found the only one on page thirty-seven and removed it. Ah well!

But I believe, though previously unrecognised by myself, that there was a latent gifting that I had never acknowledged, nor was likely to, through lack of personal expectation. For reasons known only to God, he brought this to light, and I believe (at least, I hope!) that he has used my preaching to benefit others. When I say, 'to him be all the glory', that is not mock piety, but the genuine feeling of a grateful heart. Certainly for me there has been training, demanding study and constant careful preparation, but what has not come naturally, God through his Spirit has made possible. That is what God wanted to do for Moses. It is what he did for Paul. And it is what he can do for you.

6

I am a sinner:
David's story (part two)

The girl who sat in my study looked awful – not ugly you
understand just awful. She was one of my young people at
church who was home from university, and I have her perm-
ission to tell her story. At vacation time all seemed well. She
appeared to be the happy Christian girl we had always
understood her to be, but in fact she was living a double life.
When she was with us she was a Christian, at university
anything but. At church she never missed a service, sang all
the songs with gusto, and seemed at peace with the world and
herself. At university she was sleeping around and living a life
in complete contradiction to all that she claimed to be. Some
people can live like that indefinitely, but not our friend in this
story. Finally, everything caught up with her, and here she was
now in my study looking awful. I asked her which of her two
lives she wanted to live; the choice had to be hers, as clearly
we are not in the business of forcing people to be or do
anything. 'I want to be a Christian,' she said.

I spoke to her about repentance and forgiveness, but she could not accept it. It was too easy, she said, and God would never forgive her. Over the course of several meetings I tried to explain as well as I could the grace of God for sinners like us, but gradually her sorrow turned from despair to illness. Unable to accept forgiveness and blaming herself for her condition, she slipped into a food-related illness so serious that I knew she needed professional, medical help. I will take up the story again later, but as I talked with her I was reminded of David – yes, the same triumphant King David of Chapter 4 who himself fell into terrible sin.

I am not going to imply that this chapter will be easy either for you or me. It might even be controversial. There are many Christians today who because of past overt sin in their lives feel discounted from being of any service to the kingdom of God. It might be that they feel themselves to be disqualified from ever being used by God again. Or, as sometimes happens, it is the Church who has declared such to be inappropriate for any active Christian service and that they are finished in terms of Christian ministry. Either way, the result is that tragically there is a vast number of wasted lives in our churches today. But what is more likely, though, is that such people have despaired of themselves, Christ and the Church, and have ceased to be active Christians at all.

Neither is this situation always just. Certainly there is such a thing as church discipline. To bring David to repentance he had to be faced with his sin and its consequences. However, it is true that the Church is less tolerant of some sins than others – with sexual sin being a particular anathema. Often the Church has had to cope with the critical, censorious and hypocritical, the gossip and troublemaker without any hope of discipline or even censure. But have some sexual problem, and the Church comes down on you like a ton of bricks. While I am warming to the theme, you will notice that I intentionally used the word 'overt' in a previous paragraph for of course there are people even in high-profile positions of Christian responsibility only because of what is *not* known about them. There is a hidden story line that they fear might come out. So it was with David, until he was told, 'You are the man.' One can imagine that he never had a care in the world until his past caught up with him.

If I am arguing that we must take the seriousness of all sin into account, I am not arguing that the effects and conse-quences of sin should be discounted or ignored for it brings suffering to individuals and anguish to the whole Church. When long-term lifestyles are revealed that are clearly contrary to biblical standards of behaviour, then the whole Christian constituency becomes disillusioned and angry. But does this mean that someone who falls lower than the standard that we should expect is therefore debarred from future responsibility or service? The answer is yes and no, and if you find that confusing then I think David can help us.

The story is well known of course, but doesn't improve with the telling. Perhaps the best way to come to it is through Psalm 51, a narrative so intense and so painful that you could imagine it had been written in the writer's blood. Nowhere else in the Old Testament do we find such a sense of sin, and hardly anywhere else in the Bible is repentance so intense or restoration so complete. If we didn't know David's story, we would describe this psalm as poetic, over-stated and even hypocritical. But it was no hypocrite who wrote this psalm, for David meant every word of it.

David's sordid tale is recorded in 2 Samuel 11 and 12, and it reveals David as an adulterer and a murderer, which should be enough to be going on with. Seeing Bathsheba from his palace roof, he wants her for himself. Unfortunately, she has a husband who David conspires to get killed in battle. Now of course we could make a plea in mitigation. Bathsheba was no innocent, and I suspect when she bathed in sight of the palace roof she was thinking about more than the bathroom décor. Perhaps. But whatever the circumstances, David must take responsibility for himself. There is no escape in blaming others for the sins we commit ourselves.

And what about the murder of Uriah the Hittite? Perhaps we can come to David's help here as well. He did not kill him with his own hand, did he? He *could* have come back from the ambush alive, couldn't he? No; David's conversations with Uriah display cant and calculation. The instruction given to Joab that he wanted Uriah dead means that murder was compounded by hypocrisy. There is no escape for David here either.

Perhaps a better line of mitigation for David as with other characters of history is to remind us of the time in which they lived. There is no point in imagining that David was living by New Testament norms, in the first place. There were concubines around the palace, and anyway it was a cruel age.

Sometimes John Calvin is criticised for being at least culpable when the civil authority in Geneva burnt a heretic. But in an age when even in Britain all sides of the religious divide burnt people almost at a whim, perhaps it is surprising that they only burnt one man. And what about Oliver Cromwell's military excesses in Ireland? As a fan of Cromwell, I instinctively leap to his defence. What he did is what any other military commander of his age would have done in the circumstances. However, I think it is important to say that, whatever the age, Calvin was wrong, Oliver Cromwell used an excess of force in Ireland, and David was a wicked sinner.

Why is it important to say this? Let's go back to my broken friend in my study for a moment. She could have said everyone was sleeping around at university. She could have said that her standards are typical of the society in which she lives. She could have said . . . but she didn't. When Nathan confronts David, when the reality of his crime is brought home, David does not try to excuse himself. 'I have sinned against the Lord,' he cries. Of course, he had also sinned against Bathsheba, and even more so against her husband. He had sinned against his office as king. God had removed Saul for much less. But at the end of the day, or the end of the night for that matter, all sins are against God and will have to be accounted for before him one at a time.

We live in a time of confused morality and it is creeping into the Church. The norms of the world are becoming to a degree permissible, or at least less shocking than previously. My children are fascinated that I was a teenager in the Sixties. They are surprised when I can sing along with the Beatles, aghast that despite being conversant with the pop music of the era, somehow for me the Sixties might never have happened. Had I been a Mod or Rocker? No. Had I taken LSD? No. Was I influenced by Flower Power? Hardly, for though I was a child of the Sixties, all my shirts were white, and all my attitudes a reflection of Christian norms.

But the Sixties affected all of us, even though we did not realise it at the time. The new morality somehow became assimilated not so much into our behaviour, but into our thought forms. We lost the ability to be shocked. What was shown in the cinema and on television that was thought controversial then has become accepted as normal now. Instead of there being blacks and whites in the areas of abortion, homosexuality, sex before marriage – in fact, almost any ethical subject you can name – things have become a muddy grey and this attitude has crept into the Church.

Situational ethics is no crime when biblical morality is brought to bear on the norms of society today in a way that is relevant and authoritative. The Ten Commandments still have a bearing when they are understood as being pertinent to men and women today and are described in language they can understand. Contextualisation is a vital exercise for a preacher who has something to say to modern society and address the situations that people are facing now. Nevertheless, God does not change, nor do his rules of behaviour described in the Bible, and to disobey those rules and fall short of his standards is sin, and David was a terrible sinner. So that's that then, David is finished – or is he?

Of course, there is not a Christian minister worth his salt who would not preach that there is forgiveness for the foulest sinner. We sing:

The dying thief rejoiced to see that fountain in his day.
And there may I, as vile as he, wash all my sin away.

But that is not the point here. Is there sin so heinous that it debars one from overt Christian ministry? Are we right to say, 'God cannot use me for I have sinned'? If we say no – as I want to – it must be with certain caveats. But please let me press on with my argument before you dismiss me as a legalistic bigot.

There is one thing we can say for sure: that whatever the disqualifying sin, David must have committed it. I would agree with this statement but for one thing, for in his penitential psalm David says amazingly, 'Then I will teach transgressors your ways, and sinners will turn back to you' (Ps. 51:13). 'Oh no you won't!' say some sections of the Church! But there are two obvious inferences in what David says. First, that David anticipates that God will use him again in a teaching ministry, and second, that God will bless that ministry by changing the lives of others. And if that's true for David, then it's true for everyone else, for God is consistent in his dealings with people.

Yet we are uneasy nevertheless. If one section of the Church appears hard and unforgiving, then another seems to have no concept of church discipline and apparently will tolerate almost anything. Which is right? And what should be our attitude to others and, more important in the context of this book, what should be our attitude to ourselves if we have passed along a similar route to David?

Now it is important that we understand that I am talking of something a little more than the fact that we are all sinners. For while that is undoubtedly true, and we must not forget it, at this point I am speaking about some monumental event, some moral catastrophe that has brought not only the wrath of God upon us, but the approbation of our fellow Christians. As with David, we are talking about something pretty sordid or dishonest.

If you read Psalm 51 again you will see that David is not so much concerned about a spiritual hiccup, but the whole guilt problem. He is not trying to make light of what has happened, for he is as broken as Humpty Dumpty and nobody could put him together again. He is so smashed that only the amazing grace of God could make him whole. Unless you understand this about David's plight, you will never understand the wonder of this psalm.

The trouble is that the words of David have become so

woven into the fabric of the language that they sound not so much desperate as beautiful. All this cleansing with hyssop business has a ring to it, especially when sung as some majestic *Missa Solemnis*. But that is not how it was with David. His sin was the biggest problem in his life and tarnished everything. When he said, 'his sin was ever before him' he meant it, for it was continually gnawing away in his mind like a dog with a bone.

Quite clearly, David could not deal with this problem on his own. Uriah could not forgive him because he was dead, and David could not forgive himself – and nor did he deserve to. So David turns to God, for there is nowhere else to go. Yes, he has sinned against Bathsheba, her husband, his office as king, and himself, but the bottom line is that he has sinned against God. 'Against you, you only, have I sinned' (Ps. 51:4).

The effects of this sin could not be clearer for he feels dirty (v. 7), he longs for joy once more (v. 8), he feels physically crushed (v. 8) he has lost the sense of the presence of God, and his only hope is that God might forgive him. 'Have mercy on me, O God' (v. 1). What if God were to do the impossible thing and 'blot out' his sin by his great love? My broken friend in my study would say no, that would be expecting too much.

Recently my wife and I were in Japan for its Keswick Convention. I asked the people there what was the greatest word in Japanese and they replied *megame*, which means grace. It sounds beautiful in any language. For seven happy and fulfilled years I was the senior minister at Bethesda Ipswich. The wonderful emphasis of that place was the grace of God. That unmerited initiative of God whereby he loves us in Christ, not for anything that we have done, for we have nothing with which to impress God, but because of his grace revealed in the cross. Somehow the word 'grace' used to roll around the roof of that wonderful building. Somehow grace came echoing down the centuries to meet us again. But is 'Grace' an amazing girl, as some imagine the song to mean, or a theological truth without personal relevance as some seem to imply? Or is it the love of God for me?

The grace of God did not start with the birth of Jesus. The cross of Christ was its greatest demonstration, but not its beginning. 'Have mercy on me, O God, according to your unfailing love; according to your great compassion,' pleads David. But hang on a moment, surely that is too easy for God and David. To say 'Let's just forget about it' won't quite do. What reason did David have for thinking that God would forgive him, and on what grounds? It is a hard question.

God had to show David what sin and its consequences meant. David needed to be shown that he was the sinner. He could not blame anyone else but himself. God did this through his prophet Nathan. Nathan comes to David and says, 'We have a problem.' You probably know the story Nathan told, but just in case you don't, it went something like this. A rich man who owned many flocks held a dinner party with roast lamb on the menu. But instead of killing one of his own sheep he took the pet lamb of a poor man and killed that. David's natural sense of justice was outraged and declared that this dreadful man must die, whereupon Nathan says to David, 'It's you! You are the man.' For the first time ever, David faced the truth about himself and, stumbling into the presence of God, he brings not a plea in mitigation, but a cry for mercy. Not something like, 'She shouldn't have been bathing in sight of my roof.' Or, 'She knew what she was about in tempting me.' Instead it was, 'Your judgement is right for I know my sin.'

David also knew that being religious would not solve the problem either. 'You do not delight in sacrifice, or I would bring it' (v. 16). David would have been very religious; he could have brought a thousand sacrifices if it would have helped. As the hymn-writer puts it most powerfully:

> Not all the blood of beasts
> On Jewish altars slain
> Could give the guilty conscience peace
> Or take away the stain.

If anything was going to be done to meet David's desperate need to be forgiven, God was going to have to do it. And this is what happened. 'For God so loved the world that he gave his one and only son' (John 3:16). But how does that help David who was born hundreds of years before Jesus?

What Jesus achieved on the cross travels forwards in time to me and backwards in time to David. Just as the floodlights at a football match send shadows in all directions, so the light of the love of God revealed in Jesus goes forwards and backwards in history, and around the world. 'God demonstrates his own love for us in this: While we were still sinners, Christ died for us' (Rom. 5:8).

If you wondered why this dreadful story of David was ever recorded, it was for this reason. If God could forgive David, then he can forgive me. Paul described himself as the worst of sinners because he believed he was. I think I am a pretty bad sinner too, in fact I know I am, but it was for sinners that Christ came.

Let's go back to my study and my friend, who by now I was strongly advising to seek medical help. In a way it had all been my fault. I had been a sort of Nathan in this girl's life.

God had taken a sermon I preached and had shown her the truth of her sin. Now, try as I might, I could not get it through to her that just as God forgave David, so he would forgive her through what Christ had done on the cross in her place.

Things had gone from bad to worse and guilt was spoiling everything. I will never forget the scene. Her hair hung in front of her bowed head like a curtain. I prayed quietly to myself, 'Lord, I am frightened for this girl, she is in a dangerous state and I can't get through. Please help me.' There was a piece of paper on my desk and I asked her to write down her sins. She scribbled away furiously. After a while, she handed over the piece of paper with a defensive shrug. But I gave it back to her. 'Your sins are nothing to do with me,' I said, 'but I want you to go through that list asking God to forgive you and I will pray for you at the same time.' After a while she said she had finished. There was not a hint of joy or peace on her face. I took the paper, tore it into as many pieces as I could, walked down the corridor to the lavatory, and flushed those bits of paper away. When I came back her face was radiant and she said, 'They've gone, my sins have gone!' It was an enacted parable to show what happens when our sins are put 'on Christ', when he pays the cost of our sin rather than us, when God's anger falls on him rather than me; when my sin is washed away in his blood. Through repentance and faith, my young friend's sins were gone.

Apparently David had everything. He obviously had personal charisma, for his people seemed to love him easily. He made and kept friends, as the Jonathan story illustrates. Clearly, he was a man of genius displayed in music and poetry. He was a hero in war and, as with many soldiers, so I'm told, was successful with women. Obviously he was rich. But none of this counted for anything when he thought he was going to lose his relationship with God. It begs the question as to whether there is anything more important than being at peace with God. And to recover that he was given a broken spirit and a contrite heart (Ps. 51:17). But was his expectation of a restored ministry granted to him? Did he once more teach transgressors the ways of God? Was he again used by the Lord to recover sinners?

You will have wondered at the reason for my prevarication about restored ministry for such a sin as David's. It is a sensitive matter as to whether, when a person in spiritual ministry falls short in some public way, they can be restored to where they were before. This is difficult for me because it is the position of some of my closest friends, and could one day be my situation too. If it shocks you that I should say that, then let me remind you that the Bible says that we must be careful lest we fall as well.

Quite clearly, the whole of Psalm 51 implies that David was restored in the service of God. But I guarantee he never walked on the palace roof again, just in case there was a Bathsheba Mark II bathing nearby. You see, there needs to be grace linked to common sense. Just as you would not ask a reformed kleptomaniac to work in a sweet shop, it would neither be wise nor fair, I suspect, to ask a converted paeodo-phile to teach in the Sunday school. That would be plain daft, if not criminal. If a repentant thief asks for ministry, could there not be another job other than counting the collection?

Does the same principle apply for the Christian leader who has committed adultery being asked not to be in a one-to-one counselling situation? Perhaps it does. I stopped in-depth counselling of the opposite sex many years ago, for I had come to realise that such a responsibility carried with it real temptations. It seemed wiser to build a qualified team of mutually accountable people around me for that sort of responsibility. Almost invariably it has been in the context of counselling that some of my friends have got into serious difficulties.

But are we expected to be harder than God is himself? Peter was called back into ministry. The one who denied his Lord, on his confession of love, was told to feed Christ's sheep. Within certain self-imposed disciplines, grace can recover and equip those who the world counts as finished. And that is the phrase I would like to underline: *self-imposed disciplines*. As God, through his Spirit, helps us to know ourselves better, we will begin to understand what is appropriate or unwise in terms of public ministry.

To say 'God can never use me for I have sinned' is a statement that doesn't tell the truth. It is a lie of the devil. Both the Bible and experience contradict that fact. In essence, David says to us from the pages of the Bible, 'If this is what God did for me, why can't he do the same for you?' Sense and maturity might say that we will not put ourselves again in the place of our failure; in fact, our resolve in that regard may be the proof of our repentance. God in his mercy forgets sin that has been dealt with, and if it were possible so should we. The next best thing is to keep clear of the situation where it all started to go wrong previously.

On one occasion in my ministry a lady came and told me about a specific sin that one of my leaders had committed. This sin was of such seriousness that I thought I ought to take some action. So with fear and trembling I went to see him. I asked him if it was true. Yes, he said, it was true. But it had taken place some twenty years previously. He had confessed it before God, his wife and the leadership of the church. He believed on the authority of the Bible that God had forgiven him, washed his sin away, and remembered it no more. But this lady *had* remembered! In Christ there is not only truth, but also 'grace and truth'. And there should be both in the handling of ourselves and others.

7

I feel as though everyone is against me:
Elijah's story (part one)

One of the problems about being the father of four daughters is that mother and daughters tend to gang up on you. One thing more than any other proves this to be true. Let me explain. After sliced bread, the next greatest 'thing', I believe, is the TV remote control. It allows you to whip around between programmes and catch up on the news, all at the same time. The trouble is that it causes a riot with those watching *Neighbours*. The remote control and I have almost caused the outbreak of the third world war. To be in a minority of one is to feel that everyone is against you. Now when I have complained about this mass intimidation (as I have done several times over the years), *they* say that they never gang up on me. Rather like Elijah, I must have imagined it, I suppose.

Will you please forgive me if this chapter is particularly directed to Christian leaders? But please read it, for it might help you to understand what makes us tick and why we can be such a difficult set of people to get on with.

Recently I had the privilege of writing a foreword to my friend R. T. Kendall's book on Jacob. I pointed out that all of us identify with some Bible characters more than others. For instance, as you will have already gathered, until writing this book I have never got on too well with Joseph and I have consigned Elisha to a similar fate. Despite there being many parallels between Elijah and Elisha, the latter will not appear in this book (not that he will lose too much sleep about that) and to my knowledge I have never preached a sermon on him. For some reason, I can't get on his wavelength. So why Elijah? Somehow, he seems to be my sort of man. What is more I have realised why, for Elijah was a loner.

I have always found it strange that people imagine I am a gregarious man, for I am not. Certainly I have learnt to maintain social norms and to fulfil the justifiable expectations many have of a pastor, but standing at the door shaking hands, the everyday pleasantries, and the inevitable cups of tea have never come easily to me. I have built up a few close friendships, but I am never at ease at conferences, house parties or with the necessary overnight hospitality that an itinerant preacher needs to receive from so many generous people. Give me a good book, or a day at Lord's cricket ground, or the chance to catch up on a film, and I am the happiest man in the world. Over the years my wife has learnt full well how to deal with this trait of my personality, and although we love each other's company, she knows when to build in space for me to be alone.

But for such a personality there are penalties of introversion, leading sometimes to depression. Added to this, misunder-standings and misapprehensions grow, caused by the inability or reluctance to test one's thinking and reactions against those who would have an objective view. I believe that Elijah was such a man, and this was the reason why he believed that everyone was against him. When Elijah came to the misguided conclusion that he was the only faithful follower of Jehovah in Israel, it needed someone to say to him, 'Don't be so stupid – there are at least seven thousand others who have not bowed the knee to Baal.' But for Elijah, that 'someone' did not exist – and that was dangerous.

As is so often the case with the loners of this world, Elijah could rationalise his problem. As he sat by his brook at the Kerith Ravine, what did he have to do to pass the time? He had no book to read, no radio to listen to, no CDs to play, none of those things that help to make life so good. One must presume that he lived totally with his thoughts, and that for me is not so much dangerous as suicidal. It goes something like this. A memory is dug up from the subconscious. The story is re-told. 'What did he mean when he said . . . ?' 'How should have I replied?' Before long I have worked out what I *could* have said and how the put-down line *might* have been more adroitly delivered. Of course, past pains are re-examined, past disasters re-lived, and old hurts resurrected. For me the result is a sleepless night and the onset of that touch of depression that I have mentioned elsewhere. Worst of all, it leads to the 'I am the only one left' syndrome.

Christian leaders are particularly vulnerable to this failing and sometimes for the same reason as Elijah. The long lonely hours of preparation shut up in a study, so many things that are impossible to share, the danger of having favourites and special friends, the need to be alone, are all designed to ensure that there is little cross-fertilisation with others. If that is true of modern leaders, how much more true it was of Elijah.

There is much talk today of support structures for those in leadership: somewhere where a leader can let it 'all hang out' and it can be told as it needs to be told. But you will be surprised if I tell you that I believe such support groups to be of little value if they are a mutual admiration society, a tut-tutting with each other's aggravations, a rationalisation of each other's weaknesses, and an endorsement of each other's views. What a leader today needs is something more than a friend. That is why ministers fraternals, social gatherings for relaxation, study groups, house fellowships or spiritual retreats, though valuable in themselves, could be counter-productive in this scenario – even dangerous perhaps. For me at least, to be locked up in the quiet of a retreat bedroom could be the very opportunity for my deformed thought patterns to run riot.

What is needed is someone close, who has the leader's best interests at heart, who is prepared to test thinking, disagree with wrong conclusions, rebuke misplaced trust, and censure conclusions that spring from wrong thought processes. This is to put somebody under a heavy responsibility, but every leader needs empathetic support from those who could give it. Fellow deacons will not do, for they will be implicated in the cause of the concern. A fellow elder is too close to the problem. A ministerial associate, or someone in shared responsibility, is probably as bogged down with the troubling situation as the one needing the objective support. It has to be someone else.

That is why a deacons' meeting can be a very lonely place even though you are surrounded by friends. Every set of deacons I have had have been supportive of the work I have sought to lead, and have been understanding of the rather eccentric man who was their pastor. I would not still be in the ministry today if that had not been the case. But it is not like that for everyone. And even for those blessed like myself, we too need someone outside of our immediate situation to give insight, counsel restraint, and engender perspective.

A minister known to me was once explaining to his church meeting why he felt it to be inappropriate to sell alcohol at their forthcoming fete. His ministry was on the line; he carefully tried to explain the reason for the stand he had to make when a section of the meeting got up and walked out with the explanation that it was time for *Colditz*, a then popular programme on television! That might be extreme, but it is hardly surprising that he felt lonely.

I do not know what sort of leadership you are in, but if you work alone you will need support, and if in a team then there must be the painful realisation that teamwork can be claustrophobic and there must be opportunity for expressing yourself outside the intimate circle. It will have to be faced that you just might be the cause of the tension in the group as much as anyone else, and that they might need a break too. For everyone to benefit, there must be some outside point of reference. Over the years I have sometimes been invited into these sorts of tensions to be an honest broker, but invariably it has been too late. There had been nobody to bring another perspective or to distinguish the wood from the trees.

The problem of Elijah that I seek to describe is different from loneliness, but not totally dissimilar. Not many leaders are lonely as such, being overwhelmed as they are by people. What they do lack are people who understand the unique pressures that leaders face. People truly empathetic in this regard are few and far between. All of us, at some time or another, lack the ability to identify with the pressures of living in a manse or vicarage. Sometimes we forget the tension that results from working with young people who have no interest in spiritual things. We are not mindful of the frustration of teaching a Sunday school class when every impression given by the parents suggests that it is not important. It is hard being the only Christian in a family, at college, or in the workplace. Of course, the dangers of loneliness are not unique to clergy or anything like it. But Elijah's problem was different from being on his own, although it contributed to it. Let me explain.

There are occasions when we are called to stand alone whether we like it or not. The Bible is riddled with such occasions. Daniel faced his lions' den alone. 'Dare to be a Daniel, dare to stand alone', we used to sing. Stephen had to face his accusers alone. He was placed in the pit where he was stoned to death – alone. Jesus himself 'suffered and bled and died alone' for he found no one to comfort him.

To be the only Christian in a family can be very lonely. To be the only believer at work can sometimes make one feel very vulnerable. To be at school and take a stand for what one believes to be the truth in a hostile environment takes great courage. Scripture is fully aware of this and so many of the promises come into play: 'Never will I leave you; never will I forsake you' (Heb. 13:5), and 'And surely I am with you always' (Matt. 28:20), etc. But my problem, like Elijah's, is a problem of my own making. It comes from a situation, usually self-manufactured through circumstance or choice, which finds that thinking and understanding is untested and lacks the balance of cross-fertilisation with others.

One of the major reasons for some of the high-profile calamities among Christian leaders that sadly occur all too often is lack of accountability: someone being told candidly that they are wrong. Most leaders do not lack friends, but when there is a word of censure or restraint they turn on their heels and walk away, for who needs that? The answer is, we all do. Which of course begs the question as to where all this fits in with Elijah.

Elijah's persecution complex was out of kilter with reality, but in his circumstances, what could he have done about it? Certainly there was nothing that Elijah could do about being alone by the stream – therefore God fed him and provided for his every need. One can quite imagine that he did not have too much in common with the widow of Zarephath, and to simply have company is not always the answer. Nevertheless, Elijah does meet this shadowy figure called Obadiah, who was not related to the prophet of the same name (1 Kings 18:1–15). This man could have made all the difference to Elijah.

I cannot agree with some commentators who criticise Obadiah as being compromised by being part of the court of Ahab. I ask you! It is exactly these sorts of people who are needed in significant roles within the corridors of power. I hope and pray for all our sakes that our political leaders have some Obadiahs around. We are told that Obadiah was in charge of Ahab's palace, a high-profile, dangerous and lonely job if ever there was one! But he was a brave man too, for while Jezebel was killing off the Lord's prophets he hid a hundred of them in two caves and, what is more, kept them supplied with food and water. That is quite a ministry performed by a courageous and godly man. Of equal importance he should have been a check on Elijah's muddled thinking.

Three times Elijah says that he is the only faithful one remaining. He informs the prophets of Baal and the Lord (twice!) that he is the only one left. Obadiah is the living proof that Elijah is wrong, but he would not listen. This godly man tells the deaf prophet that he has served the Lord since he was a youth and that also there were those hundred prophets safe in their caves, having a whale of a time free from danger, free from having any relevance to society whatsoever.

Everyone in leadership should have an Obadiah, and one of the most important ministries today is to be someone like him, for here is the sort of person leaders need around them. Someone who carries responsibility, is wise in the world, and exercises godly influence. I am always grateful for those in the City, or in the fields of education, law and medicine, who have been able to help me within their respective disciplines to beam light on my wider agenda. It is people like the Obadiahs of this world who can so often bring wisdom and objectivity to bear on the rather structured and regimented thought forms of those in spiritual leadership. I thank God for those who have taken me out to lunch – often a very good one – or to a day's cricket or sailing – anything, in fact, that removes me from my habitual environment and gives me an opportunity for objectivity in my thinking on life in general and my ministry in particular.

But none of this is to belittle team ministry and joint enterprise. Because of my personality I have never found this easy, but that is not to say it is unimportant. God sent Elisha to guard Elijah's physical, spiritual and mental recovery so that he did not subside into his old ways of introversion (1 Kings 19:15–21). When Elijah found Elisha he was ploughing in a field, for God will never call an idle man or woman. The ministry is such bloomin' (family word when we were not allowed to swear but wanted to) hard work! The mantle that Elijah threw over Elisha's shoulders is, I am told, a symbol of adoption and was a call to share his life and ministry. Elijah had so much to give and receive. Those who have shared ministry with me as associates and staff have become lifelong colleagues and friends. We have all learnt from one another.

One complemented the other, made up for what the other lacked, and defended the weaknesses of the other. I am sorry to go on about this, but it is important. Jesus sent out his disciples two at a time.

But the shared agenda I enjoyed with ministerial associates could not really have that objectivity that we all needed for we were all immersed in the same agenda. I met my wife at Bible college and we have enjoyed a shared ministry, but one's partner cannot always be the impartial reasoned voice that we need. Two men have played the roles of confidant and counsellor in my life.

When I was minister in Bournemouth, my church was not only blessed, happy and growing, but it was a generous church. When I attended a deacons' meeting on one occasion, I found them already in session. Seeing that this was not allowed, it could mean only one of two things – either I was in trouble or they were discussing an increase in stipend. In fact, it proved to be neither. Believing that my young family was outgrowing the manse, they agreed that the church should buy another. Not only that, they thought it would be nice for us to go out and choose it, which we did. While we were on sabbatical leave in America the church family decorated the house from top to bottom. However, just a few months later, unanticipated and uncoveted, a church in Ipswich called us to be their minister. For seven long weeks that invitation burnt a hole in my desk, as it lay unanswered. I knew that the deacons I loved and trusted would be united in their objection to our moving, and disbelieving that this could be the will of God. I needed help.

David Abernethie, who had been my own pastor and subsequently a valued friend, prayed with me and talked it through. We prayed together at the top of a multi-storey car park in Chesterfield. Scripture says that 'where two or three come together in my name, there am I with them' (Matt. 18:20). It was then, despite the disbelief of others, that I came to understand the route that God had planned for our lives. Without the two of us praying on that occasion, the rest of my life would have been totally different.

Many people know that I have a close friendship with R.T. Kendall, the minister of Westminster Chapel in London. When I lived in London, we met almost weekly; and we still meet socially with our wives whenever it is possible. That friendship provides the opportunity for relaxation and fun. There is no pretence when we are together. The sharing of insights, the discussion of Scripture, ideas for preaching, confession of need, and sometimes quite violent arguments on those matters of doctrine and practice over which we disagree, are all commonplace. It's called friendship. But more than that, it is accountability, cross-fertilisation, and a check and balance system for which we will ever be grateful. I have no doubt that is the sort of relationship that Elijah and Elisha enjoyed together as one was a mentor to the other.

And if you think that is a little far fetched, I can push it even further! More than his relationship with Elisha, Elijah imparted something of his know-how and experience to theological students starting out on their ministries. There are hints in the story of a 'school of the prophets', for they feature in the story of Elijah being caught up into heaven in 2 Kings 2. Just what this school was is not clear, but we read of such in regard to Samuel and of course Elisha. My theory (totally unsupported by anyone!) is that the prophets that Obadiah hid in caves were from just such a theological college. They were all incarcerated together, perish the thought, and perhaps Elijah taught them on their release.

That might be a pipe dream, but there is nothing like interaction with others to keep one's perspectives balanced. Why do so many, whether in a Sunday school class, youth club or a house group, have to learn by their own mistakes, when those who have been before them could have shared and given of what they had both received and learnt? In the rough and tumble of interaction there is little opportunity for the sort of morbid introspection that can be so damaging, and which nearly brought Elijah to total collapse. I wish it had been longer, but for a while I gathered together young men in my church early on a Saturday morning for a time of sharing. We talked about pressures, theology, calling and a whole host of things pertinent to where they were in their lives. These men became not so much my members as my friends, and a close affinity was maintained afterwards. By definition people who share are not alone. People whose insights are tested by debate do not lose perspective.

Elijah's latter days of ministry were strikingly different from the lonely days at the onset. For one thing he was never lonely. Elijah had to live in fraternity both with Elisha the prophet for the next generation, and perhaps in a community with others of like calling. There is one lesson that Elijah had to learn, however painfully. He was not the only one left serving the Lord, and instead of everyone being against him there were others serving God too.

The final years of Elijah seem quiet, contented and fulfilled. His end was of course unique and glorious. Instead of everyone being against him, he finally discovered that God was for him and wanted him home.

8

Nobody likes me: Jeremiah's story

Two young snakes were hurrying home for tea when one turned to the other and asked whether they were poisonous snakes. 'Why do you ask?' came the reply. 'Because I have just bitten my lip,' said the other.

Jeremiah must have felt the opposite of that snake. If only he *had* bitten his lip, then all would have been well with him. To quote that well-known mix of metaphors, it must have seemed to him that every time he opened his mouth he put his foot in it. But speak he must. He had no alternative, for God had called him to be a prophet. Now that calling went back some considerable way, for God said to Jeremiah, 'Before I formed you in the womb I knew you, before you were born I set you apart; I appointed you as a prophet to the nations' (Jer. 1:5).

It is a strange weakness in our personalities that when we grasp some distinctive truth we hang on to it like a dog with a bone. When I was a student I came to an understanding of

God that made me believe that God knew me before I knew him. And that he was looking for me before I was looking for him. To come to this understanding is of course a great comfort for it means that I was neither an accident of birth, nor lucky to be a Christian, but that I was part of a wonderful plan. The trouble is that some take one particular truth on board and they think of nothing else. There are so many 'one agenda' Christians around. I don't want to argue about God's grace for me, I don't want to go to conferences about it every week, or read magazines that speak of nothing else. Neither do I want to cut myself off from other Christians who do not see it quite as I do. All I know is that, as with Jeremiah, unless I had been convinced that God knew me personally and had given me a particular call to be his, I would have given up long ago.

Paul put it like this, 'In love he predestined us to be adopted as his sons through Jesus Christ' (Eph. 1:5). Now don't get too worried if you can't understand the long word 'predestination'. Perhaps no one understands it fully. What I know is that Jeremiah could not have kept going without the complete confidence that God had known him before he was born and called him to be his prophet. That is a comfort if you feel that nobody likes you. Let me give you a poem that was not written by Jeremiah, but by Edward Shillitto:

> Ere suns and moons could wax or wane,
> Ere stars were thundergirt, or piled
> The heavens, God thought on me, His child;
> Ordained a life for me.
> The Love of God for me began
> Long before I became a man;
> Before my lips could speak His Name,

Before from out the dark I came!
Within His mansions I was known
Before He made a Cross His Throne.
When not a seer with Him had talked!
When with Him not a saint had walked!
When melt in clouds man's hidden ways,
Deep in the dim eternal days,
His eyes, across time's troubled sea.
Went peering forth in search of me.

It wasn't that Jeremiah wanted to be disliked. He was not like those stupid people who seem to go round upsetting people on purpose. The problem was that the work God had given him to do did not agree with what the people or their leaders wanted to hear. Jeremiah has often been described as the weeping prophet, and his name has become synonymous with being something of a wet rag. The *Chambers Dictionary* contains the word 'jeremiad' and its definition is 'a lamentation: a tale of grief: a doleful story', I would not wish to be remembered for any of those things.

Let me tell you a little about the man. Jeremiah was born about six hundred and fifty years before Christ, three or four miles north-east of Jerusalem, and quite clearly he was a reluctant prophet. Not only had he no appetite for the message he had to give, but – rather like Moses – he felt he had no gift to deliver it. 'I do not know how to speak: I am only a child' (Jer. 1:6). By saying he was only a child, I suppose he meant that he was not eloquent or experienced enough for the job that God wanted him to do. For me, perhaps the most frightening thing I could imagine would be to find myself in a job I was incapable of doing, of being promoted beyond my capabilities. But God says to Jeremiah, 'Do not be afraid of them, for I am with you and will rescue you' (Jer. 1:8).

I suppose what I want to do here is to exercise a sort of rescue mission on behalf of the Jeremiahs of this world, the people whom nobody likes. If people, ordinary people, don't seem to like me, why should this be and what's to be done about it? Perhaps, rather like having bad breath, it's our own fault. Or quite the reverse, perhaps it is a cross we have to bear because of the role God has asked us to play.

Jeremiah ministered at a time when there was a political struggle for power. It had been going on for years between the Assyrians, Egyptians, Chaldeans and Babylonians. Judah was a pawn in the game, hardly of any significance in the machinations of power. Israel in the north had already been taken into captivity and now the net was closing in on the southern kingdom, the last remaining part of the Promised Land still intact. Into this fast deteriorating situation comes Jeremiah.

Jeremiah's father had been a country priest, and it is in the country that he would have liked to remain for, quite clearly, Jeremiah did not covet that high-profile ministry to which he had been called. The king at the time was a man named Josiah. He was only eight years old when he came to the throne, but now we are told (Jer. 1:2) he is twenty-one, having already been king for thirteen years. And I suppose all was doom and gloom around the court. I suppose things spiritually were at a low ebb. No wonder Jeremiah had a rough time of it standing for truth. Well, *no* actually. Let me explain.

About five years after Jeremiah began his ministry there was a high priest called Hilkiah who made an incredible discovery during building work being done on the temple. (It is a fascinating read in 2 Kings 22.) To put it into his own words, he says, 'I have found the Book of the Law in the temple of the LORD' (2 Kings 22:8). Shaphan, a secretary, told the king, in words that I think sum up perfectly the religious ignorance of the day, 'Hilkiah the priest has given me a book' (2 Kings 22:10). Apparently he had no clue what the book was. This reminds me of a story, supposedly true, that was told a few months ago of a girl who went into a jeweller's shop to buy a gold cross for a chain. The shop assistant got a tray of crosses out of the window and asked, 'Do you want a plain one or one with a little man on it?' It would be sad if it were not so pathetic.

The result of finding the Law of the Lord was something like a revival. There was certainly a reformation and there was given this wonderful endorsement of the kingship of Josiah: 'He did what was right in the eyes of the LORD and walked in all the ways of his father David, not turning aside to the right or to the left' (2 Kings 22:2). So what was the problem then? As a man of God, why was Jeremiah not everyone's favourite rather than being hated? The reason was this. Although it was not a ministry that Jeremiah coveted, he was called upon by God to preach for forty long years a message of coming judgement.

Let me round off the Jeremiah story as quickly as I can. This sensitive man came under the full glare of criticism; he was physically ill-treated and openly abused (incidentally, Josiah was dead by now). Growing ever lonelier by the year, he lived long enough to see his prophecies fulfilled when Babylon captured the land. Rather than he himself being taken away into captivity, he was left behind in the shattered country that was Judah and tradition has it that eventually he was stoned to death. So ended a ministry that none of us would have coveted or sought to emulate.

Things had been going downhill for some time prior to

that. Chapter 26 of Jeremiah tells us that he was threatened with death, chapter 37 tells us that he was thrown into prison, and chapter 38, the final ignominy of all, that he was put down a well or cistern. If ever anyone had reason to think that nobody liked him, it was Jeremiah.

Now there are similarities and several important differences between some of the characters we have been looking at in this book. For one similarity, you might say that Elijah thought that everyone was against him, and so did Jeremiah. Wrong, for there is an important difference. When Elijah thought that everyone was against him, that he was the only one left, he was wrong – absolutely wrong. That is far removed from Jeremiah. His problem was not depression, or misunderstanding of himself and his situation. Because Jeremiah was faithful to his calling from God, the reality was that no one *did* like him. In today's parlance, Jeremiah was for real, and his reality was the death of him.

As we look at the strange story of Jeremiah, for strange is what I find it to be, one comes to the painful realisation that he was in greater danger from his own people, the people he ministered to, than from their enemies, the Babylonians. Jeremiah's ministry was not accepted, his motives were misunderstood, his character maligned, and his veracity questioned. To say nobody liked him was an understatement – they *loathed* him, believing him to be a traitor. To put Jeremiah down a well was as cruel as it was cowardly.

In one of the most famous and beautiful pictures in the Psalms, David speaks of being in a pit (Ps. 40). In that picture of spiritual darkness, he cries to the Lord and patiently waits for him. David says that God lifted him out of the mud and mire and gave him a firm place to stand. More than that, the Lord filled him with joy, and put a song in his mouth. It is a deeply moving picture of salvation. But Jeremiah's story was no picture. As I have said, Jeremiah was for real.

What I want to speak of now is equally real – rare, thank God, but definitely real. There are some who out of obedience to the call of God discover that serving him is to be in a situation of pain and rejection. This pain and rejection of which I speak is not from the enemies of the gospel, or the powers of darkness, but such people are injured in 'the house of their friends'. The people of God inflict the suffering. You might reply, 'I do not believe you.' So be it, but I know what I say is true.

There have been pastors who have cried themselves to sleep because of the persistent and insidious criticism that they have received. There are some leaders who have lived almost at starvation level because they have been unsupported financially by those who were in a position to do so. On one occasion I was sitting at the lunch table during the break in a series of special meetings. The conversation, for reasons I cannot remember, was about ministers who outstay their welcome. 'So how did you get rid of him?' came the question. 'We starved him out,' was the reply. Now I do not deny that ministers outstaying their welcome can be a problem, but to starve him out? You would not do that to a dog.

Of course, this Jeremiah suffering – if I can be allowed to call it that – does not only happen to ministers and pastors. To be on any sort of Christian pilgrimage can be to know rejection, not from the world, but from within the family, from our brothers and sisters in Christ. It would be impossible for me to describe every circumstance or enter into the experience of all, but there will be many who read these pages who will say, 'That's me.'

Now there are two ways I want to look at this, both rooted

in the experience of Jeremiah. One is spiritual and the other is practical. How does God support Jeremiah who has suffered so much in his name? God tells Jeremiah that he knows him and has set him apart to be a prophet (Jer. 1:5). People might hate him, but he is loved and chosen by God. In fact, God says, 'I appointed you as a prophet.' When we have that sense of being God's appointed then we can legitimately ask, 'If God is for us, who can be against us?' (Rom. 8:31.) It is to him that we will have to give an account, not to people.

When you appoint someone to do something for you, then you guard and defend that person. It is a golden rule, for it is the only honourable thing to do. Sometimes I have asked someone to do something for me, perhaps a member of staff, and it has not been done well – in fact, it has been terrible. But in public one says nothing other than 'thank you'. The time for sorting it out is in private afterwards. That is how God is with his appointed. He defends those he has commissioned into his service even though they often fail.

Now of course if you ask someone to do something for you it is best to ensure that they are trained for the job, for otherwise they will most certainly make a mess of it. This is what God did for Jeremiah. We read these very moving words, 'Then the LORD reached out his hand and touched my mouth and said to me "Now, I have put my words in your mouth" ' (Jer. 1:9). If it had been Jeremiah's own words that had got him into so much trouble, we would be less tolerant of him. But they were not his own words, but the Lord's, for God had chosen and equipped him for the work he must do. Jeremiah is like two other great servants of God who suffered in the Lord's service. Peter said, 'we cannot help speaking' (Acts 4:20), and Paul said much the same, 'I am compelled to preach. Woe to me if I do not preach the gospel!' (1 Cor. 9:16.)

The ultimate tease for Jeremiah would have been if God had left him in the lurch and turned away when his servant was suffering because of his name. But the promise of God to Jeremiah is for everyone who has been called by God to do something, however small, for him. ' "Do not be afraid of them, for I am with you and will rescue you," declares the LORD' (Jer. 1:8). If ever you make time to read the book of Jeremiah all the way through, and I admit it is quite hard going at times, you will discover that this was Jeremiah's secret – he was never afraid for he knew God was with him.

Now we turn to some practical considerations and they are important. I want to ask what we can do for those whom we recognise are suffering in the way that I have described. If they are injured 'in the house of their friends', is it not reasonable to expect love and support to come from a similar quarter? And secondly, if we have a sense of being disliked and ostracised, is there anything we can do about it?

When Jeremiah was put down the well, God gave him a friend. When his fellow countrymen were being cruel, when he was totally rejected and left to die, God gave him a 'saviour'. The lead-up to this event was much as you would anticipate. Jeremiah's prophecy sounded like sedition, telling the people that if they wanted to live they should go over to the Babylonians. He was accused of discouraging the soldiers and people. King Zedekiah washed his hands of Jeremiah, and they lowered him down a cistern that had no water but was very muddy, for Jeremiah sank into the mud (Jer. 38:1–6). But God provided a man whose name was Ebed-Melech.

Do you ever play the game Trivial Pursuit? It's good fun. The bad news is that there is a Bible Trivial Pursuit, which I refuse to play for the simple reason that I cannot afford to let on how rusty my Bible general knowledge is. There are some people who can in a flash tell you who Joshua's second aunt once removed was, but I am not one of them! So if you are playing the Bible version of Trivial Pursuit and some of these names come up and everyone is very impressed that you know them, you will then thank me. Ebed-Melech, who has heard of him? It is true that he will never feature high up on any *Who's Who* list of the Bible, yet he achieved something of the greatest importance. Out of an act of bravery and love he saved the Lord's prophet from a dark and dangerous place. Could there be many things more important than that? Is there any service you could give that could be greater?

There is something very touching about the scene. Old rags were thrown down the cistern to protect Jeremiah's armpits and no less than thirty men pulled him out. Is this just a story from some distant age? In my eyes, a footnote of Bible history becomes something of the greatest significance. Sometimes in this book I have spoken of the trial and heartaches of leadership and problems in ministry. Perhaps some have asked whether there was anything that they could do that was significant. Well, it all depends on what you call 'significant' I suppose. How about being another Ebed-Melech, someone who sees it as their calling to support, love and encourage the Lord's servants? I have mentioned elsewhere that encouragement is one of the gifts of the Spirit. The significant thing is not only to have a gift, but also to exercise it. When someone feels rejected or neglected, to have someone come alongside could be like being pulled out of a horrible pit. Please God, give us people like that.

One last thing and this could be difficult. Some people, even Christian leaders, are not liked because they do not deserve to be. To put it bluntly, they are not very nice people. I am sorry to have to write that, but it is true.

Perhaps all of us have a rather poor regard of ourselves. Christina Rossetti put it like this:

> God harden me against myself,
> This coward with pathetic voice,
> Who craves for ease and rest and joys.
>
> Myself, arch-traitor to myself,
> My hollowest friend, my deadliest foe,
> My clog whichever way I go.
>
> Yet One there is can curb me myself,
> Can roll the strangling load from me,
> Break off the yoke and set me free.

I find that rather beautiful, and it is an honest view of self. Many of us do not like ourselves very much, and I think that is reflected in the fact that we apparently do not want other people to like us either. That could be the only explanation for our behaviour sometimes. But that is wrong – very wrong.

Jeremiah was persecuted for being faithful, not for being cussed. He did not go out of his way to upset people. Some Christians are rude, some are unkind, some are critical, some are . . . and so we could go on. I think that for those who are genuinely being made like Christ, they are assimilating his characteristics. He was gentle with people, good, kind and forgiving. To have the mind of Christ is to seek not only one's own interests, but also the interests of others. The attitude of Christ was one of self-emptying and sacrifice.

You know Paul's famous chapter on love – 1 Corinthians 13. I was once told that we would only understand it if we put Christ, who *is* love, into the text. Let me demonstrate what I mean. Jesus is patient. Jesus is kind. Jesus does not envy, does not boast, is not proud. Jesus is not rude, is not self-seeking, is not easily angered, keeps no records of wrongs. Jesus does not delight in evil, but rejoices with the truth. Jesus always protects, always trusts, always hopes. Always perseveres. Jesus never fails.

Do you see what I mean? The greatest gift is love, and Paul commands us to seek that first. And when we do, rather than no one liking us, we will become ever more like Christ. And remember, not everyone 'liked' him – far from it, in fact. But far better to be owned and loved by God than to have the passing praise of other people.

9

I suffer from depression:
Elijah's story (part two)

I read the following in the letter columns of *The Times* and it made me laugh out loud:

> The American statesman Adlai Stevenson was describing the reminiscences of some Catholic missionaries in Papua New Guinea, reflecting on the progress they had made after 30 years' hard work on the local tribes. He quotes the optimism of one priest who, despite the disappointments, remarked that at least 'on Fridays they eat fishermen'.

Elijah must have felt like that man yet worse, for apparently he had nothing at all to show for his ministry. There had been a mighty triumph for the Lord on Carmel, but now there was so little to indicate that it had ever happened. True, fire had fallen from heaven, the prophets of Baal had been demon-strated as powerless and had been slain, but for what? Here is

Elijah running for his life from Queen Jezebel and Ahab is still the major political power in the land. No wonder Elijah is depressed.

If I say that I have something in common with Elijah, sadly it is not a ministry that can call down fire from heaven or be the agency in national revival. I wish that it were. My identification with Elijah is a tendency to depression, which does not sound nearly so impressive.

Please note that I said *tendency* to depression. Depression comes in various forms. There can be clinical depression, which is a serious illness that needs professional treatment. There is also depression that is caused through circumstance. We perhaps have a valid reason to be depressed because of sickness, unemployment, marital tension or whatever. My slight depression is none of these. It happens unexpectedly, and for no apparent reason the entire world seems grey. I become under-motivated and my work rate goes down drastically. I find concentration difficult, and the only solution in human terms is to slog on until the cloud lifts.

Where Elijah's undoubted depression fits in with all this I am not sure, for I suspect that his condition described in 1 Kings 19 was a mixture of all the depressions I have described above. It certainly made him want to die, which sounds like clinical depression, yet its immediate cause was due to contrary circumstances. The remarkable thing is that when Elijah's situation is described it has a very modern ring to it. What is beyond debate is that, at a stroke, Elijah is moved from being the human agent in one of the spiritual triumphs of history to personal defeat. He moved within hours from the place of power and blessing to the desert of depression and despair, and of course this begs the question 'Why?'

There were several reasons, and although they have been

documented before they are worthy of consideration now. It is obvious from Jezebel's report to her husband Ahab, describing the amazing events that had taken place on Mount Carmel, that too much emphasis was placed on the role of Elijah. In fact, God is not mentioned at all! Certainly Elijah was pivotal to what had taken place, but he did not imagine for a moment that he alone was responsible for calling down fire from heaven. We need to constantly remind ourselves that that is the work of God alone. Jezebel attributed everything to the secondary cause. If I were to dig a garden (unlikely), I would not get too excited about the spade. Certainly a clean and sharp spade is important, but the spade itself does not over-excite us. We don't say, 'Thank you, spade' or 'Well done, spade'. It is the person who does the digging who gets the credit, and who for the sake of this illustration is me. One of the major causes of depression among Christian workers is taking to ourselves what belongs to God.

Modern-day evangelicals are particularly remiss in this respect. We look at a big personality; we weigh gifts, take note of appearance and charisma (with a small c), and generally give too much credence to those supposedly human attributes when the accent should be falling upon God, his work and his glory.

If you ever learn New Testament Greek you will discover that over the very beautiful characters that make up the alphabet there are various squiggles – they are called accents, and for some reason it is important to get the accents in the right place. The Reverend Frank Fitzsimmons, one time famous Greek lecturer at Spurgeon's College, preached on the occasion of his becoming President of the College Conference. The title of his sermon was 'Getting the Accent in the Right Place'. It was a memorable sermon, powerful, relevant and important, and I have never forgotten it. When in the things of God the accent falls on us rather than on him, we are going to get into serious trouble sooner or later. 'Not I but *Christ*', 'For me to live is *Christ*', 'That I might know *him*' is where Paul puts the accent. As someone once said – and it must have been helpful or I would not have remembered it – the letter 'I' is proud, straight-backed and shoulders out, while the letter 'C' is bent over and humble. (Oh well, take it or leave it!)

It is surprising, even nonsensical, that we have a weakness to take to ourselves what belongs to another, for if it all rests on me I will either become proud or physically and spiritually broken. Pride is the ultimate disqualification from being used by God because he will not give his glory to another, and being emotionally broken in this sense means that God can't use us anyway. Elijah, down and out in the desert, is no good to anyone. There has come about a startling change for this great prophet, so dependent upon God, so attentive to his voice. God faded out of the picture to be replaced by Jezebel.

Elijah's reaction to the threat of Jezebel that he has twenty-four hours to live is as odd as it is unexpected for he runs away. Of course, Jezebel is a cruel, calculating, dangerous woman; in fact, she is one of the famous bad women of history. But just previously Elijah had stood alone before the prophets of Baal, who could have lynched him in a moment. But there is something very typical here.

Now of course I have never had anything like the experience of Elijah, but I too have always been more frightened of individuals than congregations. Constantly, one person or another has been the focus of my disquiet and trepidation. Why do we not learn our lessons? One day when I was in the sixth form at school I threw a piece of chalk at a girl (after heavy provocation, of course – *she* had thrown chalk at me!).

To my horror, the chalk flew over her head, out of the classroom door, and into the deputy head who was outside in the hall playing the organ ready for morning assembly to begin. As I was towed off to the headmaster by my ear, this was my one consolation – they can't kill me. Neither did they – quite. Nevertheless, however we rationalise it, there are those whom we dread. The thought of them makes us groan, the prospect of meeting them becomes a nightmare. Everything grows out of all proportion. That is how it was with Elijah at the thought of Jezebel. Apparently the only solution was to run away, and a prophet on the run is in deep trouble. In fact, I have seen it argued, although I don't agree, that God never used Elijah in quite the same way again.

To have a false view of one's own importance is a chronic weakness for those of us in Christian service. 'I am the only one left', moaned Elijah, you will remember. Wrong. There were 7,000 others who had not bowed the knee to Baal. When we begin to think of ourselves as indispensable, then we are in trouble. Of course, we would not *say* such a thing, but we *feel* it: 'I am the only competent one around here', 'I am the gifted one', or worst of all by far, 'I am the spiritual one'. All of us are prone to hero-worship, and it has a bad track record in Christian ministry. When we begin to think too much of ourselves or others, we forget that God puts his treasure into pots of clay and that he only takes lowly things so that no one may boast before him.

Of course, none of us remember this basic lesson. Sadly, I have known many a ministry ruined by pride – but fortunately I have been totally free of it myself. (Joke!) We have not been on a mountaintop as high as Elijah's, but we have our own Mount Carmels. They are recorded in our carefully worded potted histories, written for publicity purposes, mark you.

They record the conferences at which we have spoken and the countries it has been our 'privilege' to visit, because inevitably people are impressed by that sort of thing. And if what we anticipate, hope for and work for does not materialise, then we too are in trouble. Whatever the sphere of our ministry, when we do not receive the recognition we believe to be our due we grumble that it's not fair. We have been sidelined, marginalised by other go-getters and careerists. Perhaps the real reason is that we have begun to think of ourselves more highly than we ought to.

I am not sure what Elijah thought the outcome of the Carmel triumph would be. Whatever, it did not happen. I am reminded of the two on the Emmaus road: 'But we thought . . .' How many of us thought that God was going to do whatever it was we were convinced he was going to do. Disappointment leads to disillusionment, which in turn leads to despair, and that leads to the depression of the desert (and what is more, all that alliteration is mine!).

One of my major concerns with some aspects of evangelic-alism is this very possibility: leaders and people becoming disillusioned because too much is being demanded of them. If false expectations are constantly being engendered, what will the eventual outcome be? If we keep telling people that revival is coming and it does not come, or declare that this new phenomenon is some great kingdom breakthrough when it is quietly dropped within months, then there will be a major rejection of the more valid things that we have to say. Perhaps recently reported figures of church attendance indicate this very problem. There is a temptation to keep up interest by novelty and secondary considerations. It might have a short-term gain, but a long-term penalty. Nothing today is a shadow of what Elijah saw on Carmel, but within days he was in the desert. And what Elijah saw was real.

Another cause of Elijah's depression was undoubtedly the fact that he was physically exhausted. When I was a minister in Ipswich I prided myself on never having a day off. It was a big church and, other than one private secretary, there were no other pastoral staff at that time. One day I was in my office talking to someone about baptism. Looking down at my Bible, everything was blurred and the person before me had turned into two. I rang my wife and told her I was seeing double. Within a few hours I thought I was dying, and within another hour I wished that I were. Eventually I was taken into hospital unconscious, all my extremities in spasm, and with the initial diagnosis given to my wife that I was having a brain haemor-rhage. In fact, it was an extreme and rare form of migraine. The doctor in charge of me, after enquiring about my lifestyle, said, 'You cannot go on like this.' Discipline about time off and the building up of a trusted staff has meant that I have never had anything so extreme since.

After the physical and mental demands of the amazing Mount Carmel triumph, Elijah ran ahead of Ahab's chariot. We are told that the power of the Lord enabled him to do that (1 Kings 18:46), but there is no mention of the Lord's power when he then ran away from Jezebel (1 Kings 19:3). The Bible says poignantly, 'he ran for his life'. It is at such moments that the devil attacks. Our bodies are the 'temples of the Holy Spirit' (1 Cor. 6:19) and need to be treated with care and a degree of maturity. There is little doubt that when we are overtired and emotionally exhausted, then we are more vulnerable than at other times.

It would be an important, if painful, piece of research that enquired if leaders who have suffered depression, or some other personal catastrophe, succumbed at a time when they were most at risk through exhaustion. When Jesus was being tempted by the devil he was fasting in the wilderness. Then the devil came to him and tempted him to make bread from a stone. It was a particularly strong temptation suited to the physical needs of Jesus. So with us, the devil comes and tempts us at our point of need. We may be physically hungry, sexually hungry, emotionally hungry, or have any other sort of hunger, and at that point the devil comes. Jesus, having been recently anointed with the Holy Spirit, was able to overcome the devil's device, but we might not be so prepared or enabled. It therefore behoves us to be sensible as to the demands we make upon ourselves. I make the point, even at the cost of people saying, 'physician, heal yourself'. Far too many Christians are tired. Either others have too many expectations of them or, like Elijah, they drive themselves literally and metaphorically into the ground. So what happens then? You pray of course.

If there is one thing I have thanked God for over the years, it is that he has not answered all my prayers. Maybe not literally to die, but I have prayed with Elijah. 'I want out' (1 Kings 19:4). For some, it might be after years of pain, wasted years in an unhappy marriage, little apparent fruit in a ministry, or something else, but the prayer has been the same: 'I have had enough, Lord.' Without doubt, many reading this book will identify with the broken man, Elijah, wanting to die.

The great news is that God did not leave Elijah in his depression and despair. He came to him in ways that were as pertinent to our need today as to his need then. There is something so modern about this passage that it would come as a surprise if we forgot the ever-present tense of the 'I AM' of God. People often (sadly) don't change; but neither does God change (I am glad to say). David wanted doves' wings to fly away from the presence of God; Moses asked to be put to death; Jonah, like Elijah, wanted to die. But that is not God's usual way. It was servants of God then, and servants of God now, who want out. And as he was, so he is now and ever will be, the eternal I AM. Therefore do not be surprised at the relevance to your situation of God's dealings with Elijah.

There is a verse in Psalms that is my favourite and I have quoted it to people in need a thousand times, probably more. Psalm 103:14 says, 'for he knows how we are formed, he remembers that we are dust'. That is an incredible truth. God knows what makes me tick and somehow understands my deepest need. More than that, he feels for us and with us, for he is not 'unable to sympathise with our weaknesses' (Heb. 4:15). So God comes to his dejected prophet, weary from the battle with the prophets of darkness, convinced that he had failed and horribly depressed. God ministers to him where he is, not where he ought to be.

First, he gives Elijah sleep. Perhaps the nearest I have ever come to a complete breakdown was in my first year at Bible College in Scotland. Previously I had enjoyed considerable responsibility in a barrister's chambers in Bristol, but now Bible College with its various rules and norms of behaviour felt like being at boarding school. Added to this, I suffered a broken relationship that I did not handle well. I was desperately unhappy. At night I would lie in bed after lights out (you see what I mean about boarding school) and listen to the radio – foul and despicable sinner that I was, for that too was against the rules. In those days, BBC Scotland closed with a prayer that quoted the Psalmist: 'I will lie down and sleep in peace, for you alone, O LORD, make me dwell in safety' (Ps. 4:8). Somehow God's benediction allowed me sleep, which I needed more than anything else. At that time there was no

word of reproach from God (that came later), but simply sleep.
Without it I would have gone completely to pieces and would
have walked away from my calling to the ministry.

We are told that God also fed his prophet, and I am
reminded of Jesus preparing breakfast for his frightened and
failed disciples for such is his love for failures. It is so easy to
trust in the love of God when the sun shines, but it's very
different in the shadows when we have failed. I love many
of the new hymns and choruses, or at least some of them,
but I am still reminded of one that we sang when I was
young:

> Standing somewhere in the shadows you'll find Jesus,
> He's the only one who cares and understands.
> Standing somewhere in the shadows you will find him
> And you'll know him by the nail prints in his hands.

That might not be Graham Kendrick, Timothy Dudley Smith,
or even Charles Wesley, but it's still true.

The angel of the Lord speaks to Elijah, 'Get up and eat, for
the journey is too much for you' (1 Kings 19:7). It can't just
be a preacher like me who finds that rather wonderful, but
there is also something strange here. The journey to Horeb –
which means a dry desert place incidentally – could have
been completed in eleven days, I am told, by my old friend
the commentator. But Elijah took forty days and forty nights.
I must admit that Bible numbers do not scratch where I itch,
but obviously this journey time is perceived as significant
because forty days and nights crop up all over the place and
you can look it up for yourself. It certainly has nothing to do
with what I am trying to say here. It is God's provision for all
our journeys that is surely the point.

When Elijah eventually arrived at Horeb, the Lord enquired of Elijah how he came to be in this place. Like taking the top off a shaken lemonade bottle, all of Elijah's pent-up hurt and frustration came bubbling out. If this chapter has struck a chord with you, then it is a question that still has to be answered. How did you come to be here? What was the chain of events that brought you to this place? How did we come to be in the state that we are? What led us to this desert place of depression and despair? So many questions – but this is important. And if you reverently say, 'But God knows everything, so why does he need me to let him know?', then I will tell you that for some reason – one beyond my understanding – God clearly asks *you* to tell *him* what your need is. Constantly Jesus asks what it is that is wanted of him. To Bartimaeus, 'What do you want me to do for you?' (Mark 10:51). To Peter, 'Do you love me?' (John 21:17). Everything has to be brought out into the open. Everything has to be told as it is. 'Lord, that I may receive my sight.' 'Lord, you know everything. You know that I love you.'

Why is it that we are so reluctant to tell God what is wrong? Is it that he will find it shocking, or that *we* will be shocked in the telling?

> Just as I am though tossed about
> With many a conflict, many a doubt,
> Fightings within and fears without,
> O Lamb of God I come.

I remember once saying to someone who was depressed, 'So am I.' It shocked me as much as it did them, for I was meant to be 'the professional' around here. 'And why?' was the retort. It was a difficult question that I avoided answering, but eventually I knew that I had to tell the Lord that I, like Elijah, was running away from something.

So we come to that majestic passage where God meets with Elijah not in the wind, earthquake or fire, but in a still small voice (1 Kings 19:9–18). Surely this is one of the loveliest passages in Scripture. The last thing you need when you are depressed is to be shouted at. Certainly these mighty phenomena displayed the *power* of God, but since when have such phenomena been vehicles for the *grace* of God, which was what Elijah needed most. We read that Elijah is unmoved by the dramatic and stays in his cave, but on hearing the still small voice he comes out. It achieved what the majestic and awe-inspiring could not.

When I have my occasional bouts of depression I don't want to be jollied out of it, or to be told to pull myself together, or to hear of some miraculous event. I, along with Elijah, need to know within my inner being that God still has something to say to me. Not, please, the god of this and that, but rather God himself, quietly speaking to me by name in terms of love, hope and future.

That voice of God when it comes might be a prompting of the mind, a prod of the conscience, a memory of past blessing, or the bringing to bear of some promise. For me, it can come through a piece of classical music touching my soul, for God will use any agency to break quietly through. 'I hear thy welcome voice that calls me, Lord, to thee.' It will always be that, a welcome call.

> I heard the voice of Jesus say
> Come unto me and rest,
> Lay down, thou weary one, lay down
> Thy head upon my breast,

I came to Jesus as I was,
Weary and worn and sad:
I found in him a resting place
And he has made me glad.

Yes, there may be the disaster of unemployment, or the
shattering experience of bereavement, or the storm of a
broken marriage, or the heat of some dreadful event. All of
these can cause depression – or there may be no obvious
reason at all. Strangely, though, all of these can also be vehicles
of the grace of God, bringing us to an end of ourselves and
catching our attention. But then God speaks. And when he
does I expect it will be quietly, and in speaking quietly he
will have broken through.

10

I am living with the burden of a broken relationship: Jacob's story

I can promise you that although I have four children, not one of them is the favourite. But I do love them all equally for slightly differing reasons that I won't enlarge upon here. I was reading the other day that there is a special bonding between a child and the father who has been present at the birth. My own experience would dispute this. When my wife went into labour for our second child, it was exactly the same time as I was due to take a funeral. There was a lengthy service in church and then a committal at the crematorium. So it was with some anxiety that I made my way to the maternity hospital. Still wearing a clerical collar, I arrived at the desk and asked for Mrs Amess. 'Oh, you could not possibly see her now,' came the reply, 'she has just had a baby.' After explaining I was not the red-hot vicar making an early visit but actually the father, I was let in. And of course that child is loved equally as much as the others.

But right from the cradle Jacob suffered from a fundamental

problem. His parents had favourites. Twins had been born into the family and Isaac loved one, and Rebekah loved the other (Gen. 25:24). Nor, sadly, was that the end of the matter. As mentioned earlier, and as modern psychiatrists and psychologists confirm, the damage that is done to one generation is often passed on to the next. So it was with Jacob. He was to put his own children through the trauma of parental favouritism (Gen. 37:3). How easy it is not to learn from our own experiences. How wretched it is when we recognise our inherent weaknesses in our children.

Jacob's parents had met in rather unusual and romantic circumstances. How Isaac and Rebekah were brought together is a lovely story. If there has ever been a marriage made in heaven, it was theirs (Gen. 24). Sadly, this did not make them any better parents, for when twins were born to the family Isaac set his love on Esau, and Rebekah set hers on Jacob. Because this is of such practical and fundamental importance, because we can be so vulnerable to this weakness without realising it, I repeat that favouritism in a family is a dangerous thing, with long-term repercussions, sometimes stretching across generations.

Needless to say, Jacob's problem did not end with his parents or his children. There was tension with his brother – and not without reason! Mummy's pet is not usually one of the world's most popular people, or the easiest to get on with. At face value, Esau had been tricked out of what belonged to him. Whatever religious gloss is put on the story, there had been dirty work afoot. Scheming by a mother to further one son at the expense of the other is wretched by anyone's book (Gen. 25).

How did this potentially damaging situation come about? It would seem that Isaac was not a strong man in character or personality. There is certainly very little about him in Scripture. He seems to have been dominated by Rebekah, which is not a satisfactory basis for a marriage, or for bringing up children. Perhaps Isaac identified with Esau because he epitomised what he was not. Esau was frank, impulsive, passionate – an open-air type who lived only for 'the now'. Perhaps – and one cannot do much more than surmise at such a distance of time – Rebekah saw much of herself in Jacob, a man described as 'sound, solid and level-headed'. Sadly, as with his mother, he was also chronically devious.

What is self-evident is that here is unlikely material to further God's purposes. Surely there must have been better stock than this around for God to use. But that is the odd thing about God, he does use the most unlikely people for his purposes. The whole of Christian history seems to testify to this.

Martin Luther seems to have been a very rum character. The saintly John Wesley was not a laugh a minute. I have just read Roy Hattersley's fascinating book *Blood and Fire* (Little, Brown & Co., 1999), the story of William and Catherine Booth, the founders of the Salvation Army. That they were great people is evident on every page, but I am glad that they were no parents of mine. In fact, the break-up of their family is one of the most painful aspects of the story.

Paul's letter to the Romans makes it clear that he too was surprised by God's strange choice in using him as an instrument of his purpose. He says, in a rather startling phrase, that it was 'in order that God's purpose in election might stand' (Rom. 9:11). The encouragement in the story of Jacob is inescapable. God seems to find pleasure in using the most unlikely people, so that the glory will go to him rather than us.

Now don't misunderstand me. I am not arguing that such things as having favourites or being careless in the upbringing of children do not matter. Or that we should be purposely deficient so that God can use us. Nothing could be further from the truth for, as we will see, Jacob's inherited personality and dysfunctional family were to be a constant nightmare for him. In fact, many times it nearly blew him away completely.

What is the fruit of being brought up in such a horrid home setting? There would be constant tension certainly. And the magnification of those negative personal traits in both Jacob and Esau were to reveal themselves later.

Without going into the whole theological significance of the 'birthright' upset, it reveals just what a wretched home it was. Rebekah dreadfully maltreated her blind husband by a deception that was as scandalous as it was bizarre (Gen. 25). This was followed by the bargaining between Esau and Jacob for the birthright, which was almost equally as obnoxious. Esau only asked for what any decent brother would gladly give – a meal. It was a crazy home by any standards, yet from such emotional cripples as these God worked his long-term plan.

Before I say anything else let me assure you I was brought up in the happiest of homes, surrounded by a wider family that I still count precious. However, it was not like that at the beginning. I was born into a single-parent family going through all the trauma of marital breakdown. Tragically, such things are much more prevalent today, but in the 1940s such an event was accompanied in a Christian home by a lot of guilt. I will never forget my mother saying to me, 'Tell them that your father is dead – not that your parents are divorced.' This was perfectly true in fact, for by then he had indeed died.

What is more, the effect of my home situation seems to trouble me more rather than less as the years go by. Without embarrassing either you or myself by going into unnecessary details, my 'preacher' father failed in his temper, appetites and faith. Seeing that he never saw me or I him (the one implies the other, I suppose) and that my godly mother did everything within her power to compensate for the loss of a father in the home, it might be thought that all would be well. Not a bit of it.

As I indicated in Chapter 5, I had a poor basic education. This was largely a result of movement between schools, and I have been trying to compensate for this ever since. I am sure that opting to study for a research degree was endeavouring to say something to myself rather than anything scholastic. As long as I can remember, and increasingly, I have suffered from a sense of vulnerability that only the love of my wife, family and the support of those I have sought to pastor have compensated for. A lack of stable foundations, a dread that the story of my father might be repeated, fears too complex to articulate here, have made me, like Jacob, surprising material for the purposes of God.

So how was Jacob enabled to overcome his crippling needs both in his home environment, background and character? For starters he had a deep personal experience of God, and in the most unexpected of situations. Typically, for someone of his type and experience, there came a time when Jacob ran away from home. To put it into modern parlance, he opted out. Even for me, the pull to pack it all in and clear off has sometimes been almost impossible to resist. But all alone in the desert, with a stone for a pillow, Jacob met God (Gen. 28). He had not planned it, and certainly was not expecting it, but he received a promise from God very similar to his grandfather's. God, from an initiative of his grace, broke into Jacob's life. God's purposes had not changed. What he had done for Isaac, his father, and Abraham, his grandfather, he now intended to repeat in him. God's promises still held good even for someone as unlikely as Jacob.

Jacob marked the place where he had met God with the stone he had used for a pillow and said, 'Surely the LORD is in this place. . . . This is none other than the house of God; this is the gate of heaven' (Gen. 28:16–17). Of course, my experience pales into insignificance. But I can take you to a house in Bristol that became not only a gate to heaven, but also the gate to a completely new life that has been more than I could have ever dreamed of. Like Jacob, I discovered that there was a ladder between God and me. It was at a time when my life was beginning to come together and I was happy. I certainly was not running away from anything. I had driven home for lunch from where I was working in the centre of the city. On the way, unanticipated and in a way I cannot explain, I met God. You can give it any theological label you like, but I met with God in a way that I had not known previously. I had been a Christian since I was a child, but this was different. God had, in a personal and unique way, intervened in my life. My room at home became a Bethel, a house of God. Over the next few months there grew a sense of call into the ordained ministry.

Now I am not arguing that Jacob's dramatic spiritual experience or my more ordinary one should be a norm for everyone. When experience is made into doctrine, we are in serious danger. Whatever our experience or lack of it, what follows is what matters; clearly, there was a new determination in Jacob that was remarkable. Please don't imagine that after this initial experience of God, everything simply fell into place for Jacob.

He worked hard for what he wanted, including his wife. The name Jacob means 'fraud' and in Laban, Rachel's father, he found his match if not a namesake. The story of the disastrous wedding to the ugly Leah is one of the funniest stories in Scripture – not that Jacob found it funny! When the heavily veiled bride was finally exposed in every sense of the word, we have one of the wonderful understated lines of Scripture. 'When morning came, there was Leah!' (Gen. 29:25). That is a line hard to beat for horror and comedy all rolled into one. Having worked seven years for the wrong wife, Jacob had to work another seven for the right one. But he did. Nothing was going to deflect him from his heart's desire. Nobody will tell you that to follow hard after God will be easy. My first year of training was the worst in my life – much of it of my own making. But it did not deter me from the goal of being trained for the work I believed God wanted me to do.

If there is such a thing as righteous anger, and there is, then there is also such a thing as righteous ambition. My sister, who suffered many of the handicaps that I did through our home circumstances, also succeeded without much effort in leaving school without any qualifications. I remember vividly when we both began at night school. It was O-Level English language, I recall. But for both of us it was a start to something we believed God wanted us to do and become. She became a teacher and I a minister. It took a long time, but it was a holy ambition undergirded by the call of God. As the hymn-writer puts it:

> Just as I am young, strong and free,
> To be the best that I can be
> For truth and righteous and Thee,
> O Lamb of God, I come.

It is no doubt true that God equips those he calls, but it is also true that the call of God often involves hard work and diligent preparation. For the Lord's work only our best will do. Jacob worked hard for what God wanted him to have. Rachel was literally the mother of the twelve tribes of Israel, but she was not given to Jacob on a plate as it were!

One of the things that impresses me is the legitimate dedication that many Christians have to their secular employment. They get up at all hours, commute vast distances, work long days, and bring work home in the evenings – all to fulfil their financial responsibilities and make money for other people. But so often when it comes to investment in the kingdom of God, another yardstick seems to apply. It is the greatest puzzle to me but, dare I say it, even Christian leaders can be, to put it bluntly, lazy. If they behaved in business as they do in the church they would be bankrupt in weeks. Sadly, second-best seems to do in the kingdom.

In the parable of the talents, Jesus, at least in part, confronts those who bury their gifting rather than take on the risk of expenditure for a legitimate return. 'But I was not prepared to take the risk,' comes the lame reply, 'so I buried my treasure.' Tragic. We are not called to ministry – any ministry – for it to be the cushy number that some have made it into. If you want to make me boil, then repeat what my oldest daughter said to our dentist when she was small (*very* small!): 'My dad only works on Sundays!' Jacob was prepared to work for what he felt was his, and we should do no less ourselves.

Another feature of Jacob's pilgrimage was his preparedness to restore his relationship with God and his family. The two should go hand in hand, but sadly that is often not the case. Jacob had experienced his first life-changing experience of

God at Bethel and there he returned for his second. But before he could come to Bethel there were two appointments he had to keep. One was at Peniel, which the footnote of my Bible tells me means the 'face of God'. It was here that Jacob wrestled with God. Then, inevitably, he had to meet his brother.

Without descending into 'blessed thought' mode, there is a divine principle here. Time and time again we have to return to the cross of Christ where first we received forgiveness and reconciliation with God. That might be in a service of Holy Communion. The words of the Communion Service have this invitation to the table: 'If you truly and earnestly repent of your sins, and are in love and charity with your neighbours, and are resolved to lead a new life . . . Draw near with faith.' It might be at a time of private reflection and self-examination. Or it might imply, as with Jacob, a wrestling with God over some specific issue. Jacob met with God alone (Gen. 32), for that is how we will always meet him. Nevertheless, there was still a social problem to be worked out, namely the broken relationship with his brother and family. When Jacob came face to face with himself in the face of God, then he could face his brother, but not till then.

So it is that the conversation with God regarding Jacob's name is of the highest significance (Gen. 32:26–30). By now Jacob is a man of experience and property, but not as yet a man of God. All that is to change, but only after a struggle. The physical fight, though real because Jacob had a perpetual limp to prove it, was symbolic of the moral struggle encapsulated in the enquiry by God, 'What is your name?' Now, perhaps for the first time, Jacob was forced to face the reality of who he was: 'Jacob' (Gen. 32:27). It meant, I am told, deceiver, liar, hypocrite and thief. All that was symbolic of

Jacob's old life. But God would have him called 'Israel', which means 'he struggles with God'.

For Jacob there were several things to put right. The foreign gods that he had accumulated had to go, for God would not renew his promise to him unless they went. In many ways Jacob's life was like any life. It had been, as with many of ours, an accumulation of home responsibilities and business claims. It had also been full of tensions, hatreds and apparent injustices. 'But I am no different from any other family member,' we protest. But that is not good enough. We are not supposed to be just like everyone else. The family question has to be faced. His parents are still alive and a meeting with his brother who, perhaps rightly, considered himself to be cheated must take place.

One of the things that has surprised and saddened me over the years is the amount of family tension there is among Christians and which, unless it is addressed, will take the edge away, not only from our walk with God, but from the pleasure of life. I suppose that the only way true family reconciliation can take place is to demonstrate that we are different, that we have been changed. If we meet estranged family members with all the old hang-ups and resentments the outcome will be to set back any hope of a meeting of minds for another generation. 'But I was in the right!' 'It wasn't fair, Grandma had promised that to me!'

Sadly, it is not unknown for family tensions to be caused by 'birthrights'. Too often have I met family quarrels over legacies, who was promised what, and a green eye concerning money. It should not be. When families – particularly Christian families – fall out over possessions, untold bitterness can ensue. Such things have spoiled many a fine testimony.

What is more important: something that will rust away

and never bring real joy or to be at peace with yourself, your family and God? In case I should be accused of being too simplistic, I ought to point out that some family problems have nothing to do with possessions and money. They stem from a deep-rooted malaise such as abuse in one form or another. That might well require some form of specialised, professional counselling. But sadly, there are other forms of family tensions that should and could be addressed by a willing and forgiving spirit. This is demonstrated in the meeting between Esau and Jacob (Gen. 33). Remember that the causes of the breakdown in relationships were real, and the separation long term.

So how did Jacob resolve this curse that had haunted him for most of his life? The meeting with Esau was initially threatening, for his brother approached him with 400 men (Gen. 33:1). Nevertheless, Jacob faced his brother alone and with deep humility (Gen. 33:3), and both were important. So often it is a refusal to face issues one to one that causes things to fester and grow.

This is not only true with families, but relationships in general. So often matters that I have refused to face, put off, hoped would just go away, have proved not to be as bad as I had anticipated when they have been eventually addressed. As with Jacob and Esau, it would have been so much simpler to handle if early action had been taken. So many family problems have become intractable through attitudes becoming set in concrete because of the passing of time. I am an inveterate procrastinator, and its consequences have often been needlessly painful.

And when Jacob and Esau did meet, the reality was completely different from whatever each had anticipated with dread. 'I'll tell him when I see him' turned out to be the hug of brotherly love, the tears of reconciliation, and the almost inevitable 'how's the family?' with the swapping of presents.

But there was also reality. Reconciliation did not lead to exaggerated and false expectations of each other. Esau suggests that the two companies might travel together – in fact, live together – but there are limits. Reconciliation is not a plea to live in each other's pockets! That could well be unwise. In the final analysis, Jacob and Esau are, at least metaphorically, travelling to different destinations. Jacob is on his way to Bethel, the place where he first met God, and of that experience Esau knew nothing. Family relationships have to be protected, even fostered, but apparently Esau is still the man 'who despised his birthright', and Jacob could not alter that. So he goes on to Bethel without him.

So everything for Jacob was happy ever after? Well no, actually. Just when things seem to be sorting out and life is back on an even keel, then bereavement strikes. Rachel, his first and greatest love, dies in childbirth on a journey (Gen. 35). Bereavement will come to us all without exception. Jacob raises a stone in her memory, for this death has to be marked, made concrete, faced and accepted. Then to add pain to injury, his father dies too. But this is the wonderful thing. Genesis tells us that Jacob and Esau were able to bury him together.

Too often, and even at Christian funerals, I have had to take a service where there has been tension in the family: hurts and arguments that should have been resolved years before. Standing there at the graveside or crematorium with memories, regrets, mistakes and injustices still spoiling this difficult and enforced reunion. Family ill-will and broken relationships are grievous things. Make sure that your death is not going to underline or compound the split in your family. Do something about it now.

Having a dysfunctional relationship is obviously a major problem and difficult to address, whether it is in the family or the church. But for the one who would be used in God's family, it behoves them not to perpetrate what they have suffered themselves and to go out of their way to seek the healing of others. After all, you might have to live with them in heaven!

11

I am single, and made to feel I do not belong: Ruth's story

I have a close friend who is a professor in a branch of mathematics at one of our finest universities. My wife and I had the privilege of attending his inaugural lecture. It was on solitons, I remember. If you don't know what solitons are, then you can look it up! After the lecture I told my friend, who was also one of my church members, that I had not understood everything he had said – which was a gross understatement, for I had understood hardly anything. 'I don't understand everything *you* say,' was his reply. Now that worried me, for I believe that what I have to say – in church at least – is important and needs to be understood. In much the same way, I believe this chapter, touching as it does on areas of ultra sensitivity, needs to be clear and simple. Much has been written on the subject of singleness, much of it erudite, worthy and potentially painful. However, this is not a discussion in a vacuum but the reality that many face, and I will try not to make sensitivities worse but instead point a way forward.

The reason for the vulnerability that this chapter engenders is that so many today feel, like Ruth, that they do not belong. They feel that because of their singleness, whether it is through widowhood, divorce, lack of opportunity to build a relationship with the opposite sex, or a conscious decision to be celibate, they have no natural self-expression in the Church.

Ruth, as a child of her age, suffered from about as many drawbacks as anyone could face in Bible times – or any other time for that matter. She was a young widow with all the loss that this simple statement implies. She was a stranger and foreigner in an insular community. Added to which, she was horribly poor. Like so many who find that circumstances are against them, she could have subsided into bitterness and irrelevance. Sadly, irrelevance is the inevitable fruit of bitterness for it leaves us damaged and with tunnel vision, obsessed by the imagined or real reason for the hurt. And yet in the plan of God, rather than feeling herself to be a reject she became the great-grandmother of King David and an ancestress of Jesus. Like everyone else, in the purposes of God this lady was important.

The story of Ruth is placed at the time of the Judges of Israel, a time not unlike today in that morals were at a low ebb and religion was degenerate and polluted. Yet in the midst of this darkness is depicted a depleted family that bridges the age-old enmities between Israel and Moab and gives a glimpse of love and faithfulness overcoming bereavement and disaster. This story, written at a later time, has theological meaning beyond the scope of this book, for it speaks of Boaz as a kinsman redeemer and points to the work of Christ for our salvation. But it is Ruth, as a representative of today's lonely and disenfranchised, who interests me here.

To understand how Ruth speaks to our situation today

means knowing something of her story. Because of famine, Elimelech and Naomi, Ruth's future parents-in-law, had left Bethlehem – yes, that Bethlehem – and had gone to live in Moab, a land situated east of the Jordan and the traditional enemy of God's people. They took with them their two sons Mahlon and Kilion, who married local girls Orpah and Ruth. Sadly, all the male side of the family died, which seems a bit excessive, but life was short and hazardous in those days. The sense of sadness and loss that surrounded the surviving women is obvious if not stated. That they had grown in mutual love and regard together is clearly inferred by the grief expressed at their parting. When Naomi heard that things had improved at home, the now decimated family set out for Judah. Knowing the pressures of being strangers in a strange land and understanding some of the problems of being 'foreign' in a tightly indigenous community, Naomi encourages Orpah and Ruth to go back home. After much weeping, hugs and kisses, Orpah does so, but Ruth continues to Bethlehem with her mother-in-law to begin a new life there.

Mother-in-law stories do not abound either in Scripture or devotional literature. We read of Peter's mother-in-law, but other instances fail to come to mind. The story of Ruth is deeply moving, for despite the tragic bereavement through which the family had passed, relationships were in good repair. One must presume there had been the attendant distribution of family assets and effects that are a part of the practical process that follows death, but clearly these had been handled without tension.

Coming out of the pressures Ruth faced from her mother-in-law to return home to Moab with Orpah, she says those famous words (which were preached at our wedding incidentally), 'Your people will be my people and your God will be my God. Where you die I will die, and there I will be buried. May the Lord deal with me, be it ever so severely, if anything but death separates you and me.' Now that is moving in any age. Ruth had every reason to speak of the separation that death causes for she was a young widow. But she was determined to overcome her despair. How do I know that, you might well ask! The obvious reply is that the Bible tells me, for in an almost throwaway line it says, 'Ruth was determined' (Ruth 1:18). Here is the secret of Ruth's ultimate triumph. But all that is a long way ahead, for rather like Jesus' words to the disciples in the Upper Room, there were many things Ruth would learn that she could not bear now.

At the point of the parting of the ways from Orpah, there is not the slightest hint of hope for the future let alone triumph. It was not so much that Ruth resident in her new home of Bethlehem did not *feel* that she belonged, but that this *was* the literal truth. In her new community she would have known no one other than her mother-in-law. She could have slipped into bitterness and depression as her lot. Wallowing in her loneliness she might have become part of the flotsam and jetsam of life, not fitting in anywhere. But the Bible tells us she was determined – determined that her present circumstances should not be the end of the story.

Perhaps it was not that Ruth was determined, but that she was stubborn. Is there a difference between determination and obstinacy? Was Ruth's determination a refusal to be walked all over, to be a doormat for an unsympathetic society, a constructive resolve to make something of her life, or a denial of the docile acceptance that some today imply is what it means to be 'spiritual'? Without determination in a life already blown to pieces by disaster, Ruth's future would have been utterly wasted.

I have known a little of the determination that the story of Ruth describes. For myself, it was a refusal to accept the status quo and to make something of my life. Call it a holy ambition if you like. Some people have called it stubbornness, and I have sometimes wondered what the difference is between determination and stubbornness or obstinacy. Here are two definitions – make of them what you will. Determination is a 'conscious adherence to what is right after a careful examination of the reasons that could be given for the opposite course', while obstinacy is 'the maintenance of a position whether it is right or wrong'.

It is to ensure that Ruth is not being obstinate in deciding to go forward to Bethlehem that Naomi tests her thinking and resolve so stridently. Was she prepared to go the way of loneliness that was the road to Bethlehem, or was it a stubborn refusal to do the logical thing and go back home? As the poet asks, 'How far is it to Bethlehem? Not very far.' Neither was it for Ruth, but emotionally no journey could have been longer. No life has ever been more changed by her resolve to travel the miles into an unknown future. For Ruth, the road was longer than she could have possibly imagined. It was beyond her capacity to understand, even if she had been told, that in taking this journey she would become an integral part of the history-changing events that took place in Bethlehem centuries into the future.

In the story of Ruth it can be demonstrated that determination could also be called obedience, for the strange purposes of God were involved in this young widow's resolve to travel on with her mother-in-law. Despite the fact that Ruth personified some of the multifaceted aspects of singleness that are prevalent in the Church today, and that I want to look at in this chapter, her resolve carried her through.

The first aspect of singleness that I want to touch on is Ruth's refusal to allow the tragic death of her husband to be an excuse to subside into despair. She was resolved to face the situation that had beset her through no fault of her own – namely, the loss of her husband. To be a young widow is awful. After the initial falling in love and building a relationship, the setting up of a home and the honourable and legitimate pleasures of a normal married life, to have it snatched away is almost the ultimate tease. Inevitably, as a minister I have had to witness and support both husbands and wives who have passed along this way of heartache.

Bereavement is like an illness. It can neither be defined nor normalised. What it is for one is completely different for another, and feelings can recur in a moment. A favourite piece of music, a loved holiday destination, witnessing children growing up, a family wedding, almost anything can cause the return of the flood of emotions, the sense of pain and loss that is called bereavement. There are two alternatives that Ruth faced. Either she could return to the place associated with her loss or make a new life with her mother-in-law in Bethlehem. She was determined to do the latter, and in doing so was brought to wider horizons and new relationships that she could never have dreamt of.

There are of course other reasons for singleness apart from widowhood, and one of them is caused by the breakdown of marriage. From Christians in senior leadership, to those holding less onerous responsibilities in the Church, marital separation is spreading like a contagious disease. Over the years, people have become painfully aware of the consequences of broken relationships. It might be a church confused and disillusioned by the loss of its minister into a relationship that is a complete denial of everything that has been preached for years. It might be a husband or a wife who, after years of apparently happy marriage, suddenly finds what is imagined to be a more attractive alternative and leaves. The consequence for the one left behind is singleness. And it is possibly even more difficult to handle than bereavement because of its association with betrayal, regret, anger and sense of failure.

Another form of singleness is where there has been a breakdown in family relationships, and we have touched on this earlier. One of its consequences is feeling a stranger in one's own house or family. A hundred things can cause such tensions. A couple can fall out of love. One partner, previously a practising Christian, can abandon the faith – leaving the other to soldier on in the pilgrim way alone. An outsider can break in; a cuckoo can be born into the nest bringing resentment and confusion. Family tensions over such issues as money, who will look after Grandma, who was left what in Mother's will, jealousy. In fact, I think I have seen as many different causes as you can imagine over the years.

Families in tension find it difficult to worship together; in fact, I have known families sit in different parts of the church where they will not need to meet. They will certainly find it hard to socialise together, with times like Christmas being a nightmare. The outcome is inevitable loneliness and a feeling of not belonging. Those who seemed so close and important might as well have died for all the love, understanding and support they give. In fact, their very presence is a continual reminder of anguish and betrayal. Perhaps Ruth's bereavement was easier to handle. Sadly – although 'tragically' would be a better word – I have had to officiate at too many Christian funerals where there has been tension, bitterness, regret and guilt for past family breakdown. Despite the cost of losing her sister-in-law, Orpah, despite being a foreigner in enemy territory, despite the prospect of loneliness and poverty, Ruth was sticking with Naomi. But there are other forms of singleness that have not been mentioned that for many are as pressing as any of the above, and we must ascertain how Ruth coped with the various social and emotional handicaps that she faced.

There are many who would argue that the classic form of singleness that many find so difficult – the fear that one may never find love or lifelong companionship – is harder to bear than Ruth's singleness caused by widowhood. After all, she had known and enjoyed a fulfilled intimate relationship, even if only for a short time. Some years ago I was involved with a couple who were very much in love, but the man was dying of AIDs. Two days before he died I did all within my power to marry them, for, the young woman said, it would be so much easier to handle the future as a widow. People often know how to support marital bereavement; it engenders instinctive sympathy. Therefore it would be wrong to imply that Ruth had nobody to love her for she was loved by two men at different times and was wonderfully supported by Naomi. Nevertheless, she was determined not to be broken by her circumstances. That is the point. So at last we turn to that classic singleness which causes so much pain and misunderstanding.

There are many things that we feel we might wish to be otherwise. Many situations that we face that seem unfair, and perhaps that is exactly what they are – unfair. Singleness for either sex can be a crippling handicap to some, while to others the freedom that it allows seems preferable. But to want to be married – or, dare I say it, to *need* to be married – and never have that opportunity is a burden more than some people can bear. 'Am I unattractive to the opposite sex?' 'Is there something wrong with my personality?' 'Should I look outside the church for a partner?' are all questions that I have frequently been asked.

The problem is in part a feeling of missing out. You might well ask how I know this as a married man – I can only report what I have been told many times. Of course, it is not a universal reaction from people who are single, for some have taken a conscious decision to remain alone, believing that the benefits of being single outweigh the disadvantages of having a permanent relationship with someone of the opposite sex.

Neither does singleness imply celibacy in our secular society. But for many Christians under the restraints of biblical discipline – whether, as in the case of Ruth, it is temporary, or otherwise – celibacy is seen as a negative condition. That is a modern concept. For centuries in the Church, singleness was seen as the preferable state. Clergy were expected to be single, nuns were married to Christ alone. Sexuality was sin, and any feelings of physical desire were to be repressed. As with so much else in our day, all of this has been turned on its head. The pendulum has swung from one extreme to the other. Now there is a current view of singleness, even in the Church, that sees being unmarried as a crippling or unwholesome experience.

To be a single man, even in the Church, is to be subject to the unexpressed suspicion of being gay. To be a single woman is to imply that one must be lacking in some area of appearance or personality. It is quite true that the Old Testament focus in the creation ordinance is a presumption that 'a man will leave his father and mother and be united to his wife, and they will become one flesh' (Gen. 2:24). But as with so much else, Jesus changes all that. 'At the resurrection,' says Jesus, 'people will neither marry nor be given in marriage; they will be like the angels in heaven' (Matt. 22:30). The truth is that both marriage and celibacy are normal possibilities. Ruth experienced the joys and trials of both.

Jesus was single but he had friends who were women, and disciples who were married. He understood all sorts of states and described the crowd as his brothers and sisters (Mark 3:34) and prescribed no particular marital state as normative. The determination of Jesus to do the will of his Father came before everything else.

Contrary to modern emphasis, Paul describes singleness or celibacy as a charismata, a gift for the whole body of Christ: 'I wish that all men were as I am. But each man has his own gift from God; one has this gift, another has that' (1 Cor. 7:7). Singleness allows for mobility in service without the restraints of schooling for the children. Singleness allows for the release of wealth where there is not a family to support. Singleness allows for flexibility of time that family life does not allow.

Someone has tabulated some of the reactions that singleness seems to engender: 'She must be frustrated – forty and not married', 'Such a nice man – I wonder why he is not married', 'She has a lovely home and a good job – she doesn't need to get married'. And following the lead of the apostle Paul, 'He is important to God – it would be a waste for him to marry.' The truth is that many, because they do not belong specifically to anyone, do not feel they belong at all. It is the loss of owning and being owned that is such a major factor in the emotional life.

Ruth could have gone on with Naomi, back to Moab with Orpah – or neither for that matter, because she was single. Apparently her own agenda was the only consideration. It is this that I believe people find difficult. One day a delightful, integrated single woman was with my wife as she was ironing clothes in the kitchen of the manse. Suddenly she burst out, 'I would give anything to iron someone's shirt!' She longed to give and take, to love and cherish another, to be responsible for them, in a way that was intimate and ordinary – mundane even.

When Ruth had the opportunity to marry Boaz, she did so. Probably the majority of people would like to get married in the right circumstances. But that constant reminder to the single of the assessment of their peer group, that somehow they are perceived as deficient, is something almost too much to handle and emphasises the pain. Phrases like 'perhaps it will be your turn next', 'never say die' and 'good things come to those who wait' give the impression that the person is less than what was intended. That they do not belong to anyone and no one belongs to them. That is a feeling hard to accept.

Now please do not misunderstand me. I am not suggesting that if we stick our chins out, hide our emotions, determine to make a go of things, all will be well. Not at all. Ruth knew loneliness as she worked in the fields alone. She knew humiliation as she claimed the paupers' rights of gleaning after the harvesters had passed through. Initially she must have been sceptical, if not antagonistic, to Naomi's schemes for her to obtain a new husband. But Ruth was determined.

All of us are called to life in Christ that is characterised by love, and love needs more than one. Love cannot be expressed in a vacuum for it must give and receive; yet sometimes for a Christian that active generous expression of love is not discovered in the Church. Sometimes singleness is seen as an impediment rather than an opportunity. When what we all need, close friends of both sexes, is unobtainable or not encouraged within the 'fellowship', a sense of rejection or inadequacy is the inevitable result. But Ruth was determined to make a new life with her mother-in-law; and she was open to enterprise and a degree of honourable manipulation to achieve her goal (read the story for yourself and see if you agree with me). It is then that she discovers that life opens up for her.

Ruth could have become bitter about her circumstances. As a young woman her world had come tumbling down around her, and she might well have succumbed to self-pity. But she does not sulk, blame other people, or make other people's lives a misery. A mature Christian is one who, whatever the circumstances, through an enlightened mind and a consecrated heart, presses on. A Christian is one who, although they may not have chosen to write their history in the way it has been written, believe that God's way is best.

'Mum, I am coming with you to Bethlehem,' said Ruth. 'But you don't know anyone there,' replied Naomi. 'But I am determined to come anyway,' said Ruth. 'How will you live?' asks mother-in-law. 'Where will you live?' 'I have made up my mind, I am coming with you to Bethlehem,' is the reply.

I wish I could positively say that there would be a Boaz at your Bethlehem – if you wanted one, that is! But there is something about Ruth that I love. Delivered from doubt, distrust and disillusionment, she affects those with whom she comes into contact in a way that is positive and constructive.

Sadly, when people become bitter about the ramifications of life and feel that in comparison with others they have had less than they desired or anticipated, their walk with Christ suffers. This, almost invariably, is the consequence. One becomes angry with one's lot, angry with the Church – for that is often the arena where one's frustration is highlighted – and, eventually, angry with God himself. There is need for determination here for all of us. 'I have decided to follow Jesus, no turning back' we have sung. 'Be faithful, even to the point of death, and I will give you the crown of life' (Rev. 2:10) is the promise of Christ himself.

I can imagine that some will be sceptical about all this, with the following implied questions: 'So the Ruth pattern means that I will never be lonely, frustrated or sad?' or, 'If I follow her philosophy of determination, will it make everything come right for me?' Nobody can promise any such thing. But it is clear that her determination confirmed Ruth as important in the plan of God. She became one of the human ancestors of Jesus. For those who are determined to put Christ before circumstance, for those who hunger and thirst after righteousness, theirs is the kingdom. To have the kingdom is to have everything and more. Not bad for someone who did not belong.

12

I have a broken marriage:
Hosea's story

I have to confess that other people's love stories are not quite
what I would choose to read about, or go to the theatre or
cinema to view. But sometimes they are difficult to avoid,
particularly on Sunday mornings. Let me explain. Most
Sunday mornings I am driving to preach somewhere. It is
then that Classic FM, a channel that normally makes good
company, broadcasts a programme called *Classic Romance*. The
idea is that a true love story is read and then linked to a piece
of music. Usually the stories are of the most inane type
imaginable, and I would advise you to avoid the programme
like the plague. I suppose the Classic FM stories told are
important to the ones who wrote in with them, yet it is having
a need to share them that I cannot understand – or listen to
for that matter.

So why did Hosea feel the need to tell us his marital disaster
story? Why does he feel the need to embarrass us in this way?
Let me try to explain, but first with a caveat.

Now of course I am not suggesting that there are no complications here. The whole question of divorce is one of my concerns in this chapter, even though it is generally agreed that Hosea was never divorced. The whole matter of what leadership roles are available to those who have experienced marital breakdown has been discussed at great length elsewhere. It is beyond my remit now, and I will but touch upon it. My concern is that a frightening number of people in the Church today have either been converted after a broken marriage or have had to endure the agony of a broken marriage as Christians. Each, in one way or another, are asking, 'Can God use me?' The answer to that question is yes, because Hosea experienced the agonies of marital breakdown and he was a prophet.

The story of Hosea's marriage is one of the most moving in Scripture. Through the years there have been arguments by commentators about the story that is recounted in the first four chapters of Hosea. Is what we read allegory or did it actually happen? It is almost as if the idea of a Bible prophet having an adulterous wife was too shocking to contemplate unless it was dressed up as a picture. Read the story for yourself and I anticipate that you will agree with me that the pain described is not picture language or metaphor, but the expression of a man passing through unending emotional torture; for although Hosea's wife was a depraved woman, he refused to let her go. He would not divorce her. Let me explain.

To put it bluntly, Hosea married a woman who, if she was not a prostitute in the classic sense of taking payment for sex, might as well have been. Her behaviour, we are told, was *like* that of a prostitute, which is much the same thing. That Hosea refused to let her go is the whole point of the story, for unfortunately his marriage epitomised the broken relationship between God and his people.

George Matheson, we are told, suffered a broken engagement and wrote that beautiful hymn 'Oh love that will not let me go', and if Hosea had been looking for a title for his prophecy that could have been it. The more Hosea's wife went out with other men, the more he loved her. Despite her fixed resolve to sleep with as many men as she could, Hosea provided a home, and gave her that which she least wanted – his love. Of course he warned her, pleaded with her, cajoled her, but her response was to humiliate him the more. And in response, he loved her still more.

Now don't misunderstand me. Hosea did not condone his wife's behaviour. It made him angry almost beyond words. If you read the book you will discover that the writer seems to jump all over the place. He darts from one thing to the next. It is a picture of a man agitated, so taken up with his driven concern over the behaviour of his wife that he can hardly maintain consecutive thought. He is as desperate as that. The behaviour of his wife pervades everything. Adultery is vile to him, as also is the unfaithfulness of Israel in departing from the Lord and turning to idols. To God, idol worship is a sort of adultery. It is giving your love and affection elsewhere. This picture of adultery seems to touch everything in the book.

So God packs in his relationship with Israel even as Hosea puts away his wicked wife. But that is wrong on both counts, for neither God nor Hosea does any such thing. They are hurt, heartbroken and certainly angry about such unworthy behaviour, but nothing can stop them loving even when their love is spurned. Hosea 2:2 might be presumed to be speaking of divorce, but in fact it speaks of the prophet's determination to win back his adulterous wife by love. For the Lord has commanded Hosea to, 'Go, show your love to your wife again, though she is loved by another' (Hos. 3:1).

Adultery is a terrible sin, but it is not an unforgivable sin. I think people, particularly Christians, forget that. Although all confidence and trust can be broken down, although there is a sense of betrayal coupled to a righteous anger, even adultery can be forgiven by the grace of God. What is more, I have seen it happen – although often it does lead to divorce. And not only adultery; cruelty, desertion and the irretrievable breakdown of a marriage can all bring about a separation that is final, apparently unreconcilable and leads to the break-up of a home. Is there any way that God can use someone who has suffered this ultimate tragedy? Can a modern-day Hosea be used by God?

'I won't allow divorced people to be members of my church,' said the pastor. One of the heads of his denomination was rather knocked out by this. 'Do you think people who have gone through a divorce need Christ?' he asked. 'Yes.' 'Would you preach the gospel to them?' 'Of course.' 'If they were converted, would you baptise them?' 'Yes.' 'Would you then allow them to join the church?' 'No.'

The denominational head personally reported that conversation to me, and it reveals a strange logic. All Christians are agreed that divorce is a terrible thing. Divorce is contrary to what God had in mind when he commanded Adam and Eve to 'become one flesh'. Divorce is against every biblical picture of what marriage is and signifies. I am reminded of the bishop who, when asked what he thought of sin, replied that he was against it. So too, with much the same blanket response, the Church is against divorce. It is as simple as that, for divorce is a terrible thing against the plan and purpose of God. But having said that, you have not said everything.

So what is strange about this logic, it could be asked, seeing that we are seeming to endorse the view of the pastor mentioned above. Just this. The local church is the tangible expression of the universal Church, into which we who are Christ's are brought by faith in his work on the cross. That Church is the body of Christ and each one is a part of it, whoever we are. Paul is quite clear about this for he says that 'you are the body of Christ, and each one of you is a part of it' (1 Cor. 12:27). But the pastor above says, 'But you can't be part of *my* church.' I repeat: that is a very strange logic. Paul said, 'For we were all baptised by one Spirit into one body – whether Jews or Greeks, slave or free – and we were all given the one Spirit to drink' (1 Cor. 12:13). I suppose Paul, if he had been writing today, could have added 'divorced or not divorced, separated or together', for sadly so many in the Church today are passing through this trauma.

Hosea loved his deviant wife and would not let her go. God loved Israel with an everlasting love. Love does not always end with divorce or separation, though it would be so much easier if it did. One of the strangest memories I had as a child was when my mother received a telegram and burst into tears. She told me my father had died. But why cry? I thought, seeing that he had done so many terrible things to my mother, including leaving her for another woman. The simple reason was that she loved him.

All too often I have had to witness the breakdown of a marriage and it has always been with tears. But does that mean that such people are then forfeited of any expectation of being used by God again? I think not. For myself I might anticipate that as a pastor it would be difficult to lead and teach in areas where I had proved deficient. But not all agree with me. I might feel that Paul's injunction that an elder is to be the husband of one wife might discount me from such a role in the local church if I was remarried, but again not all would agree with me. I might feel that all those who have gone through such an experience should take a back seat away from the public eye, but if I thought that, I know I would be wrong.

One of the most misunderstood passages in the whole of Scripture is to be found in Hosea, partly because it has formed a famous metrical hymn that begins, 'Come, let us to the Lord our God with contrite hearts return.' But although the sentiments were phrased in high-sounding words, that is all they were – just words. Israel piously continues, 'Let us acknowledge the LORD; let us press on to acknowledge him' (Hos. 6:3). But they did not mean it. God's reply is this: 'For I desire mercy, not sacrifice, and acknowledgment of God rather than burnt offerings' (Hos. 6:6). This is a word to all those who have drifted away from God or have brazenly turned to their own way. Are those who have suffered marital breakdown the only ones disallowed from full restoration into the purposes of God? Could a loving God restore Hosea's deviant wife? The answer is yes, as well as the crook and the thief. And the gossip and the liar. And the hardhearted and critical. And the sinner of any sort, since Jesus Christ came into the world to save sinners. If there can be restoration for David, who we have looked at already, then there can be restoration for you and me. And the one who Christ restores is the one whom he deigns to use. In the light of this who will dare to say that whereas this might be true, they cannot be used of God in *my* church?

Perhaps the costliest, most uncoveted ministry in the world is to be able to sit down with someone and say, 'I have been where you have been. I have felt what you have felt. And this is what the Lord has done for me.' Only one who has suffered in the area of marriage can say that to another like sufferer. This is the last sort of ministry that we would want, expect or covet, so much so that I trust that we will not have to exercise it. But should that be our hard calling, God will help us through.

To be used by God is not like being 'used' by people, which so often means being manipulated by others for their own selfish purposes. Being used by God means significance and opportunity in the family of God. It means having a reason to be alive and something to achieve while we yet live. It means being changed from one degree of glory to another until one day we stand perfect before Christ. And then together we will be used in praising him, the one who took hold of such unlikely people as you and me and made something wonderful out of us.

13

Things will never be the same again:
Haggai's story

One of the blessings and curses of life is memory. Perhaps the best tip I have ever received as a parent is to give your children memories. Whenever we are together as a family it is no time at all before someone says, 'Do you remember when we . . .' Invariably the memory is not of some expensive holiday, but of something quite small. When we all lived together in Richmond, way after bedtime I would occasionally say to the kids, 'Let's go up west.' We would take the car to the West End, have a drink at McDonald's, and come home. It was nothing other than something that created a memory (although it was great fun too). Every family has such memories, or at least every family *should* have them.

But the trouble with memories is that they work both ways, for sometimes they can be our enemies. There are things that we hoped had been buried and forgotten years ago that suddenly raise their heads again and everything comes flood-ing back. For me it can be passing the end of a road, a chance meeting after a service, a half-dream in the night, and suddenly I am catapulted back into some situation I had wanted to forget.

Perhaps the most insidious of these memory problems, and perhaps its most usual manifestation, is remembering not just past disasters, but past triumphs and comparing them with the present. We remember that time when everything seemed better than it is now.

That was Haggai's problem. Everything in post-captivity Israel was a poor reflection of what it had been previously. He was ministering in a situation that was a shadow of past glories. He did not need telling that things were never going to be so good again, for he only had to look at the ruin of Solomon's temple to know that. The trouble is, that is exactly what people kept telling him – once, it was better.

Haggai, like me, was born at the wrong time. Trust us, we might feel, to be ministering at a time when the spiritual tide is running out fast. Trust me, says another, to be a pastor when congregations are down, commitment on the wane, discipline in service almost non-existent, and revival further away than ever one would imagine. If we feel like this, and there are many who do, then we will discover there are striking similarities between Haggai's situation and our own.

It would seem that at the time of his recorded prophecy, Haggai was an old man. It is just possible that he had witnessed the destruction of Solomon's temple, I am told. Whether he had seen that temple or not, he had certainly been told about it again and again and again and . . . This wonder of a structure, associated as it was with everything glorious in the heyday in Judah's national life, was now nothing but a pile of ruins – and the ruins were themselves a constant reminder of defeat and failure. But now, and the date of his ministry can be ascertained to be exactly 520 BC, his ministry was to the 50,000 Jews who had returned to Jerusalem led by Zerubbabel. You can read what happened next in the stories of Ezra and Nehemiah. After an exciting start in rebuilding the walls of the city, the work had now come to a halt through opposition from the Samaritans (Sanballat and Co., you will remember). By Haggai's time the initial optimism had evaporated and all that was left were memories. Things were never going to be as good again as they were before, that much was clear.

Discouragement, somewhat different from depression, is something most of us have faced. In the words of Winston Churchill, discouragement comes like a 'black dog' day. Everything takes on a lacklustre appearance. Previously there had been enthusiasm, but now pessimism sets in. The characteristics of discouragement are always the same. Difficulties are blown out of all proportion; decisions are put off; and secondary issues become all-pervasive. Rather like a yacht taking on water, there is a danger of being overwhelmed. The outcome is similar to depression in that we want to opt out and run away, or camouflage our discouragement by seeking fulfilment in something else. All of this can be seen in Haggai.

Loss of hope or despair is, I once read, 'an unwillingness to view one's circumstances from a divine perspective', which is rather good I think. It is manifest when we begin to compare our situation with the past because, as with the temple of Solomon, it was always so much better then.

Duke Street Baptist Church, where, until recently, I have been privileged to be senior minister for a number of years, had as its first pastor, F. B. Meyer. Now that is a name to conjure with. He was the first Baptist minister to speak at Keswick, most of his books are still in print a hundred years after they were written, and his biography reveals a man of considerable warmth and stature. It must have been so much simpler to minister in Richmond, a leafy Victorian suburb, at a time when religious observance was at its zenith than now – or, at least, considerably easier. Even in living memory there have been such famous ministers as Alan Redpath and Stephen Olford, to name two who knew much blessing. But of course all statistics confirm it was *so* much easier being a minister in the 1950s than the 1990s or in the new millennium – or *was* it?

And then there is something about those names of the previous generation, is there not? There was a Victorian divine called Octavius Winslow. What a name! He preached at the induction of C. H. Spurgeon and wrote a wonderful book on the Holy Spirit. Now if I had been called Octavius Winslow, that would have been something else. I can just hear it – have you read this book, listened to this tape, been at that conference with Octavius Winslow? Or how about Lloyd-Jones, that's a great name – in fact, any name but mine. All those great men were so much more powerful, so much better Bible expositors, than anyone today: 'I can remember when the church was full', 'I can remember when we had baptisms every month', 'I can remember when Pastor Joe Bloggs was minister here. We had great blessing then', and so it goes on.

Did you hear of the minister who, in the course of a sermon, asked anyone in the congregation who had never sinned to stand up? To his amazement and disquiet, a man near the back stood up. 'Do you mean to say you have never sinned?' asked the shaken minister. 'Oh yes, I've sinned,' said the man. 'So why are you standing?' asked the minister. 'I am standing in memory of my wife's first husband,' came the reply. It has *always* seemed better before and how discouraging that is.

Yet rather than being blown away by the problem, Haggai meets it head on: 'Who of you is left who saw this house in its former glory? How does it look to you now? Does it not seem to you like nothing?' (Hag. 2:3). Well, yes, it does actually. The music, the ritual, the architecture! This place is never going to be anything in comparison to that one. And whatever our particular ministry, we have all had to face it. Whether it was the Boys' Brigade or the Women's Meeting, it has always been better some time previously. And, come to think about it, those good times were just before we got our hands on it, or so we imagine.

The first thing Haggai will not permit is a defective view of the past, for unless care is taken the past will spoil the present and pervade the future. For that is what happens if we are not careful. The past haunts the present and spoils it. It might be the cliché that puts the dampers on all initiative: 'We have never done it this way before.' It might be the empty pews or the old impressive Sunday school register, or whatever. But the result is the same, for the past wins hands down. Haggai asks us to look at the past with maturity and reason. Was the past ever what it seemed? And if it was so good, why has it handed to us such a poor legacy now?

When Joshua, several centuries before Haggai, viewed the prospect of following such an illustrious leader as Moses, God tells him quite emphatically that Moses – his undoubted servant – is dead. It is for Joshua to get on with taking the land promised to Moses, which, by the way, he never entered. The story of the march to the Promised Land is an epoch indeed. The Exodus has such a ring to it. But in fact forty years had been spent wandering round and round getting nowhere. 'Listen Joshua,' says the Lord (this is a paraphrase you'll understand), 'don't let the past get out of proportion.'

Returning to Haggai, we discover that one or two literary techniques are used to get his message across. (You can either trust me that this is so or, better still, look up the references). First, he does something we were trained *not* to do at college: he asks a series of rhetorical questions. 'Well, what's wrong with that?' you might ask, 'Everyone does it' – which is one reason for a start why we shouldn't do it. Another reason is that because we are wicked, when the preacher says, 'Shall we pray?' we almost instinctively want to say, 'No!' But in asking his questions, Haggai is asking his hearers to think it through for themselves. In effect, he is saying (my paraphrasing), 'If things are so bad today compared with the past, why are you not doing something about it?' (1:4). 'If my house is so disappointing, why is that?' (1:9). 'Who remembers what it used to be like anyway?' (2:3). 'Just because you can't pay the pastor, the congregations are going down, and there are no young people, do you think I am going to leave you like that?' asks the Lord (or words to that effect!) (2:19).

Another technique that Haggai uses is repetition. As with little children, something is said over and over again so that it will sink in. No less than four times in the first two chapters he says, 'Give careful thought.' When we imagine or imply that things will never be as they were, it is because we are not thinking the matter through. It means that we are not bothering to think. (Mark the repetition.) God has not changed, the gospel has not lost its power, the Holy Spirit is still active, and the needs of people are the same – 'think about that' says Haggai right through his short prophecy. Our responsibility is for today. Our opportunity is now. Our calling is to this generation. God has given us a rebuilding task for our day and it is time that we got on with it.

Twice the Lord says to Haggai, 'I am with you.' Once again the emphasis is on the present tense, for our God is the God of the present tense. In other words, 'I AM that I AM. Our God is for now. Now is the day of salvation, for this generation, and for this millennium.' The promise 'I am with you' is either true or it is not true. If the former, then there is little point in being wrapped up with the imagined glories of the past. God was with them and God is for us. 'So get on with the work,' says Haggai. ' "Be strong, all you people of the land," declares the LORD, "and work. For I am with you" ' (Hag. 2:4).

I am reminded of the story of the disciples who fished all night on the Sea of Galilee and caught nothing – which was surprising considering that they were professional fishermen. Jesus commands them to fish again. But they had failed before and the daytime was not the time for fishing. There had been nothing to show for their work. Yet when they were obedient to the command of Christ, the crew that had failed previously caught a vast amount of fish. Not only was it the same crew that had failed, but they fished from the same boat on the same water and succeeded because the Lord had commanded them. When they forgot about the past and were obedient to their present responsibility to fish, amazing things happened. So Haggai says to himself and the people, words to the effect that they must get on with the work of rebuilding the Lord's house. We have to start getting our priorities right. Rather than looking after our own interests, we have to build for this generation and its spiritual need by having a worthy place of sacrifice and worship. That the new temple was not a patch architecturally on the previous one is not the point. Neither was the temple that was built in Haggai's day to be compared with the one that replaced it. This new, wonderful, third temple was built by Herod the Great, but it was polluted and its services compromised by the corruption of the priesthood and its kowtowing to Rome. It is better by far to have a place of worship that may be no great shakes to look at, but where the presence of Christ is found and the power of God is seen.

There are three things that I am seeking to say about this feeling of despondency that we all face from time to time. I have tried to analyse the problem, then look at how Haggai responds to it. But sooner or later we have to do something. Haggai says to the people, 'We have to get working.' That is the biblical response. It is not theory; it is action.

Well of course that is obvious, for nothing will come without hard work, we say piously. But just as with the Jews in Haggai's day, we put it off, preferring to remember imagined past glories. We procrastinate by considering some mythical golden age.

Procrastination does not mean our intentions are not good, or that we don't intend to build, but for various reasons – some of them apparently legitimate – we put things off. There is a practical test by which you can tell a procrastinator. If ever you see pieces of written work that procrastinators have done, you will discover that they are reluctant to turn over the page. It's odd but true. As they get towards the bottom of the page the writing gets smaller, and if the paper is lined then they continue to write beneath the bottom line – anything, in fact, rather than turn over. But procrastination leads to discouragement. The work builds up, the time-scale becomes shorter, the demands more extreme. They tell themselves to get on with it, but they can't. They know they must revise for that exam, but they don't. They are painfully aware that a piece of work has to be handed in by a certain time and stay up all the night before to get it done. I know what you are thinking,

'How does this man know so much about procrastination?' One day I will get around to telling you.

Here is the word of God through Haggai. Stop living in the past, put the future into God's hands, and get on with it. And 'it' in the case of the Jews in Haggai's time was building the temple. The people were very busy, but they were busy with the wrong things. Of course, every Christian worth his or her salt is busy about something. In fact, we impress ourselves as much as other people by just how busy we are. We wouldn't be able to live with ourselves if we were not busy. But it begs the question as to whether we are busy about the things that really matter. Haggai says these cutting yet powerful words: 'my house . . . remains a ruin, while each of you is busy with his own house' (Hag. 1:9). Ouch! Haggai describes the hurly-burly of life when he says, 'Give careful thought to your ways. You have planted much, but harvested little. You eat, but never have enough. You drink, but never have your fill. You put on clothes, but are not warm. You earn wages, only to put them in a purse with holes in it' (Hag. 1:5–6). Ouch again! That hurt, for the meaning of Haggai is obvious.

We spend so much of our time doing things that do not count, and working for that which does not matter. I have known ministers spend literally thousands of pounds on books they never read. Some people go here, attend this, do that, and achieve nothing. Life has never been busier, yet apparently we are walking a treadmill that is gradually taking us backwards. Never before has there been so much available to Christians to train them for this, give them tools for that, and teach them how to do the other. And the Lord says, 'Put your effort into building my house.' If we were to do that with a will, the present would be more glorious than the past.

Haggai tells the people that they need a plan of action (Hag. 1:8). It is a detailed account of what the people need to be doing in rebuilding the temple. I am sure that if we are in leadership – any sort of leadership – we dare not drift on year after year hoping that things will get better, consoling ourselves by remembering the supposed great days of the past. Our work, for that is what it will be must be prayed through, worked out, strategies and goals set, and then we will hardly have time to be discouraged or despondent.

Rather wonderfully, Haggai in his little prophecy stops looking back and looks forward to the promised Messiah of God whom he describes as the 'desired of all nations' (Hag. 2:7). When he comes, says Haggai, the rebuilt temple will be filled with glory (Hag. 2:7). It is an incredibly exciting passage of Scripture.' "The glory of this present house will be greater than the glory of the former house," says the LORD Almighty, "And in this place I will grant peace" ' (Hag. 2:9).

Somehow everything is put into perspective here. The future is going to be far, far better than the past. God's new work will be greater than anything done previously. It will be glorious. So that is what we hope for. That is what we work for. There is something so wonderful coming 'that we would not believe it, even if we were told'. We had better be getting on with it then.

14

The person God uses:
Nehemiah's story

Let me warn you from the outset that people with a burden
are very difficult to live with. To mix my metaphors, they
suffer from tunnel vision flavoured with lashings of emotion.
Such people have haunted me through the years. 'Should not
the church be . . . ?' 'What if . . . ?' 'Did I believe that God
could use them to . . . ?' I repeat, people with burdens cause
problems for everyone.

Perhaps I had better explain what I mean by 'burden' in
this context. By 'burden' I mean someone who comes to an
understanding that God wants them to do something. Someone who, perhaps suddenly, after years of apparent anonymity
as far as they and God are concerned, senses that he is speaking
to them about something specific. Then the trouble starts.
They pester the leadership of their church with their 'vision'.
They bring dis-ease to a marriage for they talk of plans that
would shake the nest. They are prepared to leave a steady job,
change career and spend hard-earned cash for no reason other

than – to use a hackneyed phrase – 'God had laid something on their heart'. Such people are dangerous.

In this chapter I want to describe these 'dangerous people'. It is not much of an identikit of the person God uses, for we are all different. Yet we need to understand something of those characteristics that mark out people who have achieved things for God. And such a man was Nehemiah.

And please don't think that Nehemiah was running away from anything because, on paper at least, he seemed to have everything going for him. He came from a privileged family background. He held an honourable and onerous position in the royal court of Babylon. As the cupbearer to King Artaxerxes, he had the ear and trust of the supreme ruler. Scripture records the story of Nehemiah as being about 446 BC. Although others of his own people, the Jews, had returned to Jerusalem, Nehemiah had remained and there was no reason why he should not live a long, responsible and secure life. Not many of us would ask for more than that. But then Nehemiah got his burden and life was never going to be the same again. He might have been important, successful and rich, but those things do not count for much when God tells you to do something.

There is no hint in Scripture that Nehemiah is in the wrong place by being at the court of the king – far from it. It is the plan and purpose of God to have his own in significant places. Some are called to create wealth, some are in education, others in the caring professions, and some are homemakers. It must have been a cause for considerable satisfaction that there was a Jewish representation with influence so close to the king. I expect Nehemiah himself felt like that until he got his burden. How did he hear God speak? Clearly, Nehemiah's success in the secular world had not dented his relationship with God or his concern for his people.

It might have been better if Nehemiah had gritted his teeth until his burden went away, seeing that it was going to cost him greatly in the loss of personal prospects and safety. In fact, his world was about to be turned upside down. Nevertheless, there was one thing Nehemiah never doubted and that was his responsibility to do something. If only he had stayed in Babylon, he would never have heard of Sanballat and his motley crew. If only I had stayed in the law, I too would never have heard of church meetings, missionary councils and, much worse than these, those names I dare not mention.

But how can I test my burden? How can I know if it is from God? How can I know that it will not pass with time? I think Nehemiah can help us. It is quite clear that Nehemiah had an intelligent understanding of the needs and problems in Jerusalem. When his brother Hanani and others came from Jerusalem to Susa where Nehemiah was serving the king, we read that he 'questioned them about the Jewish remnant that survived the exile, and also about Jerusalem' (Neh. 1:2). He is informed that the people are 'in great trouble and disgrace. The wall of Jerusalem is broken down, and its gates have been burned with fire' (Neh. 1:3). Nehemiah's burden for Jerusalem rose from an intelligent concern about what was going on.

By 'intelligent' I do not mean 'brainy', you understand. It did not takes brains but passion to tell our church in Bournemouth that down-and-outs in London needed socks. The man in question was not without brains of course, but somehow he 'grew' this burden and was not content until we had sent away thousands of pairs of socks. Richmond is one of the most affluent parts of the country. We were therefore doubly shocked to hear that one bitterly cold winter's night two men had died from exposure under Richmond Bridge. It did not take brains, but costly commitment, to provide a hot meal on our church premises every Tuesday evening for drug addicts, AIDs sufferers, alcoholics, schizophrenics and down-and-outs. More than that, it took considerable personal courage too – for sometimes these unfortunate people were violent. Once some of our people were made aware of a problem, they researched the need and did not rest until they were doing something about it.

Am I wrong to suggest that someone who testifies to a concern for Sierra Leone should know more than where to find it on the map? That someone who feels called to counselling should be prepared to go on a course to help in what is a minefield for the unwary? Or that someone who wants to bring young people to Christ will go to the place where young people are to be found? It is as simple as that. No, not simple perhaps, for burdens are never simple.

But there has to be something more than that. One of my weaknesses is that I am a newsaholic. If I had my way, I would listen to the news at 6 p.m. on BBC 1. Then I would turn over to ITN for the news at 6.30 p.m. Moving quickly over to the splendid news at 7 p.m. on Channel 4, I would then hang on till the 9 p.m. news on BBC 1. *Newsnight* on BBC would more than help to get me through to the 11 p.m. news from ITN while still bemoaning the loss of *News at Ten*. Of course when things got difficult and withdrawal symptoms were creeping in, then teletext always helped being so close at hand, for I was watching for the football scores at frequent intervals anyway. To the charge of 'Why?' from my family, came the obvious but lame reply, 'Something might have happened.' But the person I knew with a burden for Afghanistan was interested with a minute focus on but one country and one need of a people without Christ. That burden cost her everything. Like Nehemiah, she was deeply moved by what she heard. She more than anyone I have known could have sat down and wept with Nehemiah when he heard the news from Jerusalem (Neh. 1:4).

I am desperately trying not to slip into a preaching mode, which is hard for a preacher, but I must tell you that unless you have a concern for the lost you will never be an evangelist. You must realise that unless you love young people you will never be used to bring them to Christ. One man said in my hearing that there were only two reasons why people were unconcerned about the fate of those who were without Christ. The first was that they did not believe that such people would go to a lost eternity anyway. The second was that they did not care. It is people who don't think like that who are the motivated ones, and hence the people used by God. The people I have met with a burden from God, whether it was some spiritual need or social concern, discovered that it changed their lives and their understanding of the meaning of life.

It goes without saying I think that Nehemiah prayed about his burden concerning the state of Jerusalem. Well, you would, wouldn't you! 'For some days I mourned and fasted and prayed before the God of heaven. Then I said: "O LORD, God of heaven . . ." ' (Neh. 1:4–5). I suppose what we pray about may be one of the best tests as to what our burden is. Tell me that you have a burning longing for something that you don't pray about and I, for one, will not believe you.

But of course there is yet something more before we can judge whether Nehemiah's burden was to have long-term consequences. Much of what I have written above should be true of us all to one degree or another. We can and do pray about matters of intelligent concern, and if that is the end of the matter there is little more that is expected of us. But not for the one with a burden – there has to be something more, for there comes a time when they have to *do* something.

It would have been the easiest thing in the world for Nehemiah to think that seeing that he lived hundreds of miles away he was hardly the man to be the catalyst in this desperate situation. But very soon his burden was beginning to touch him in ways that it had not done previously. 'Why does your face look so sad when you are not ill? This can be nothing but sadness of heart' (Neh. 2:2). Even Artaxerxes had come to realise that there was something up. At that moment it all comes tumbling out, for having prayed an arrow prayer to heaven Nehemiah instantly replies, 'Why should my face not look sad?' Having described the desperate situation of his people in Jerusalem he says, 'If it pleases the king . . . let him send me to the city in Judah . . . so that I can rebuild it' (Neh. 2:5). The whole matter was confirmed by the fact that 'it pleased the king to send me' (Neh. 2:6).

I suppose that if the king had said no, then that would have been the end of the matter. To use modern parlance, the door would have been shut and Nehemiah would have been released from his burden. But that did not happen. Neither could it be said that Nehemiah lived the easy life in the service of God. You can read the thrilling story for yourself, a story of opposition, setback, strategy and hard work. Nehemiah's story interweaves with Haggai's and others, for there were many who had complementary burdens coupled with considerable disappointments too. Inevitably, there was plotting from the outside of the walls and disappointment from within. Yet he continued his mission; he never stopped until his mandate was complete and his burden removed – if it ever was.

★ ★ ★

When I told the senior partner that I was leaving to train for the ministry, he said I was a fool. I suppose one can only ascertain if he was right by the criteria with which you pass judgement on my proposed course of action. That was thirty-five years ago, and in many ways the intervening years have been like the characters I have tried to describe in this book. Each year knew triumph and heartache, success and failure; this comes to all those who yearn to be the ones God uses, and I count myself alongside them. Some of God's people have completely changed history; were strategic in God's greatest plan of preparing a way for the coming of his Son, our Saviour. Most of us, though, will be a footnote (or less) in the annals of the history of the faithful.

And yet God has not changed. The people contained in this book were unknowns in their day, living in some back-water of the world, totally disregarded by those considered powerful and strategic at that time. Certainly there was a Moses who led a great people from exile to the very borders of the Promised Land. There was a David, who as king, musician and poet has made an indelible mark – not only on his own age, but today also. On the other hand, there is a Ruth whose story would not have featured as significant even in its day – or even after, were it not that her name is recorded in the genealogy of Christ. All of them, with perhaps the exception of Nehemiah, were dysfunctional or handicapped in one respect or another, all of them could have felt that they had no part to play: very little to offer in the way of gifted service. Some of them, like Jacob, had very little knowledge of having been used at all.

Yet all of them had a personal experience of God. Particularly with Jacob, yet with all of them, there seemed to be a ladder, which reached from God to where they were, touching their lives and changing them. That meeting with the Divine turned the most unlikely places and situations into the house of God and the gate of heaven. And although I barely register in comparison with such people, I too discovered that God wanted to use me. Looking back, as with them, there is an equal mixture of pain and joy, disappointment and hope. Meanwhile, we journey on in the confidence that it is God's purpose to use an equally disparate set of men and women for his purposes. And, once you know that (even if it is something hard to comprehend or explain), it is to know something that can change a life completely. For if you have caught nothing else from these pages may it be this: that whoever you are, apparently insignificant or otherwise, God can use you.